Grief-Stricken

STORIES OF ALTERED LOSS IN A PANDEMIC HAZE

A Teaching Memoir

Laurel Elizabeth Hilliker, PhD, FT
Fellow in Thanatology

ISBN 979-8-88851-307-1 (Paperback)
ISBN 979-8-88851-309-5 (Hardcover)
ISBN 979-8-88851-308-8 (Digital)

The events and the people depicted in this book are real. The loss stories shared occurred in the year 2020, during a global pandemic. The grief that resulted continues as we live out our lives.

Covenant Books
11661 Hwy 707
Murrells Inlet, SC 29576
www.covenantbooks.com

This book has a dual dedication. First, I dedicate it to the bereaved family members noted within these pages, who, with broken spirits and hearts, freely agreed to share their grief stories. I will always remain grateful to *Kevin*, *Jeff*, *Maureen*, and *Debra* for their courage, selflessness, and willingness to help others.

Likewise, I dedicate this first edition to *Blessed Michael McGivney*, a Connecticut priest who served the people of God during the nineteenth-century pandemic. He, too, fell ill and died of pneumonia in 1890 just two days after his thirty-eighth birthday. I attribute the acquisition of a Christian book publisher for *Grief-Stricken* to his intercession.

C O N T E N T S

Part II: Perseverance

Part III: Courage

ACKNOWLEDGMENTS

This work would not have been possible without the support of so many close others, especially my husband, Kevin, and my adult children. They encouraged me to keep writing and continued to ask about my progress and setbacks along the way.

A sincere thanks goes out to my close colleagues, whose work I quote in these pages. I also admire the many classic writers, specifically the journalists, academics, poets, book authors, mystics, and saints cited, who have shaped my ideas and have sparked personal and spiritual growth.

Additionally, I am indebted to my supportive La Crosse, Wisconsin, conference family, who provide me with confidence through their friendship. I would also like to thank the team at Covenant Books for their attention to detail, their patience and encouragement alongside their professionalism in helping to get this book to print.

I appreciate Ben, Amber, Nora, Jon, Melissa, and Becky for permission to share their additional tributes for the family members we lost in 2020.

Lastly, I am grateful to my many close friends who were relentless in providing various support to me through the writing of this book, namely Lin, Kathy, Laurel B., Laurene, Sr. Pat, and Mary Grace.

COVER PHOTO

There is a story in this beach scene, as it appears in the cover photo, that needs to be told. It involves my sister-in-law, Maureen, who lost her only daughter and who shares excerpts in this book and resides in Colorado. I had agreed to provide her with support by text, as that was her preference, while processing the sudden loss of Anna.

It was an ordinary day for me as I worked away, writing up north at my lake house in Michigan. Suddenly, a text came my way. Her desperate cry for help via text read, "I can't do this anymore, hanging by a thread." My heart dropped. I knew my brother Jeff, her husband, was out of town and my nephew Ben, her son, was out of the country. Immediately, I had to be on the move (flight or fight?). I was drawn to the beach, about 150 yards from my little cottage. As I ran to the lake, I thought about the message I would send back to her so that she would "hold on."

Arriving at the water, I saw a beautiful piece of driftwood. I had no idea why, but I picked up a stick, drew a big heart, and attempted to make a connection with a message from her daughter. I snapped a photo with my phone of the humble drawing, whispered a prayer, and sent it her way with a message to "pull back." She replied almost immediately with "I love this. You don't know how many times you have brought me back from the brink."

The photo-text was so meaningful to this brokenhearted mom that she had the photo printed and framed, and I decided to use it for the cover of this first edition of *Grief-Stricken*. It is a stark reminder of how even the smallest gestures of support can be lifesaving to those who are in the depths of grief.

INTRODUCTION

If you have experienced a significant loss of someone loved, cared for the dying in medical settings, or provided support to bereaved others in the pandemic years, this book is for you. If you want to understand how twenty-first-century post-pandemic bereaved individuals are experiencing loss and change in their lives, this book is for you.

We have all seen the disheartening data for lives lost because of the pandemic (over one million in the United States alone). Also, some of our family members' lives ended naturally but occurred, unfortunately, during this global pandemic. Although the cause of their deaths might not have been from the contagion, the experiences of their dying and our grief were altered in many ways.

I have witnessed numerous stories from the bereaved relatives of people who died alone or in the presence of medical providers whom they had never met. These stories of hardship impacted not only the dying but also the helping professionals at all levels and the disenfranchised family members who were not able to be present. May this book and its content equip you, the reader, with a better understanding of what bereaved individuals are processing and what they continue to need.

The writing of *Grief-Stricken* began in late fall of 2021 from the shores of one of Michigan's Great Lakes, Lake Huron. From the beach the sun can be witnessed over the water both rising and setting because of the unique peninsula location. The beautifully colored leaves that were witnessed then rapidly began falling from the trees as a reminder that the world does go on, in some fashion, even during very painful times in our lives. Life on this planet continues even when we feel as though it should stop to coincide with our feelings and experiences. The trees stood strong, yet a beautiful part of them was missing. There would be new growth, in time, at the right season.

The sound of the waves landing on the shoreline with the gentle breeze and sun against my back helped to restore some of the brokenness that loss brought my way. Because of the multiple loss of family members in 2020, and the disruption it brought, I believe that I, too, entered a new season in my bereavement and in my life.

Lake Township, Michigan, beach at sunset, 2021

I write with the expectation that the stories shared here will bring comfort in the months and years ahead for readers. In particular, this book is for those who also suffered significant loss resulting in an altered grief during the pandemic, which is ongoing.

Umberto Eco, an Italian semiotician, novelist, and philosopher once noted, "To survive, you must tell stories." Here in *Grief-Stricken,* the loss stories unfold under several themes, namely embracing change, perseverance, and courage. You will read how we held onto reasonable hope and practiced self-compassion as we learned to carry our grief. This book project has also served to help us to make sense of these deaths as we integrate the losses into larger life stories, our new narratives.

First, this goal is addressed by sharing with the reader how I view the topics of loss and change as a scholar and as a personal griever (Chapter 1). Following the first chapter, we move through the news of loss, both receiving it and delivering it (Chapter 2), and the disruption it brings (Chapter 3) along with the uninvited suffering we experience (Chapter 4).

Next, an examination of what grief can teach us through the emptiness and loneliness we feel is put forth. This chapter includes a look at the need to surrender to what we cannot change by weaving in quiet time practices and sitting with the unanswered questions in order to then contemplate the changes (Chapter 5); followed by a recognition of a transitional period, which includes a discussion on moments of awe and gratitude to allow for transformation and a new perspective (Chapter 6), eventually leading us to explore our new role through identity work and to consider rising up and out of ourselves in order to connect to and help others in our shared humanity (Chapter 7).

Lastly, a look ahead using the concept of reasonable hope as we figure out how to continue a bond with the deceased while living forward with remembrance (Chapter 8). Concluding remarks are added together with a postscript on how the chief mourners (who shared these stories of loss through excerpts) are managing as the book ends. Each chapter also provides key takeaways for the reader to consider.

Through my writing and the excerpts shared, the continued need for support for those grieving in our times is highlighted; therefore it seems appropriate to refer to this first edition of *Grief-Stricken* as a "teaching memoir." Much of what I have learned and will share in these pages comes from an array of interdisciplinary scholars whose shoulders I stand on, from my own grief experiences, and from my observations and support for close others during these past few years and in the six plus decades I have lived. However, those I consider to be the true "experts" are the bereaved themselves.

Additionally, the knowledge I gained through my studies in sociology with a concentration in health and well-being and a specialization in grief and bereavement will be weaved throughout. Recognizing the personal losses of millions of people during the pandemic years is daunting, yet I felt they should not be ignored. The tremendous loss brought great suffering but also valuable insight that need our attention and compassion.

The pages herein describe not only the working through of my own grief but also include the voices and experiences of those closest to the deceased, the chief mourners. I know that these stories do not belong to me alone; therefore, I asked my family members who were most impacted to share as well.

In part, this book's purpose is intended to bring an awareness to readers about the importance of respecting the unique and various ways in which people grieve loss. *Grief-Stricken* is not meant to be a one-size-fits-all model for everyone's grief journey, as we are all exceptional, and our grief is unique and complex for many reasons. Rather, the book aims to highlight the personal ways in which we grieve. It recognizes the challenges of grieving when the world is chaotic and we are all in need of consistent, continued, and unwavering support. Strong social connections, which are critical for our emotional well-being, were jeopardized because of the twenty-first-century pandemic.

Grief-Stricken captures the recent struggles and triumphs of my brother Jeff and his wife, Maureen, who suffered the sudden loss of their adult daughter Anna Louise; my maternal cousin (Debra) who lost her husband, Wade, after a long illness; myself and my siblings, along with the extended family, who lost our mother/grandmother/great-grandmother Anna Marie in old age and my husband Kevin who lost his only brother, Mark, to COVID-19. Numerous hardships in one year on both sides of our family, accompanied by a pandemic, were hard to bear and support.

After several months of quiet reflection on these multiple and complex losses, accompanied by lake life, clearer vision arrived. Although it is best to grieve loss together, and to have great support persons alongside you, grief also requires a good deal of self-reflection. I sensed a transformation from this experience of reflecting on the accumulated loss, both from death and the residue of fractured relationships. What was necessary work on my part became crystal clear. I had to write.

I thought about how many other bereaved individuals need help in moving through tremendous loss during these extraordinary times. I share these stories with the sincere hope that they will be helpful to others who find themselves in similar circumstances. I am confident that through the courage of those sharing excerpts of their grief stories here, the writing of *Grief-Stricken* will bring more peace our way. It has already been realized as cathartic for those who contributed excerpts, and we believe it will add another layer of legacy to the beloved individuals we lost, Anna Louise, Wade, Anna Marie, and Mark.

There has also been a strong urge felt to preserve our stories by writing parts of them down in words. Anais Nin once wrote: "We write to taste life twice, in the moment and in retrospect." We have done just that as we attempted to capture our ongoing grief as this book evolved. We construct and edit this new narrative as we move through the grief. Our hearts are grateful for being able to love the people we lost and now grieve.

To help you, the reader, appreciate our stories of loss, first you must meet these beloved family members through our descriptions and tributes. The start to the year 2020 was uneventful, until mid-February, when just before the world shut down, we lost Anna Louise, my niece. Our family came together to help our brother, his wife, and their son bear the heavy burden of the sudden loss of their daughter (and sister). Then, as we were trying to make sense of the pandemic, our maternal first cousin experienced the death of her husband, Wade, in July of 2020 after many years of caregiving. Shortly afterward, we saw our aged mother, Anna Marie, begin to fade away before our eyes, and she took her last breath in October 2020. This was followed three weeks later by an unexpected and sudden loss of Mark, my husband's brother, from COVID-19.

In less than a year, we had lost four cherished people in our family. Because of all the restrictions and the contagion, we had limited and/or questionable gatherings by some people's standards. Nonetheless, we carried on bringing honor to their lives as best as we could, given the circumstances.

We worked closely with end-of-life professionals, the "last responders," including hospice teams to keep our dying in their own homes, funeral directors, our devoted priests and chaplains along with the forgotten saints, such as crematorium attendants, gravediggers, and the cemetery crew. They are the forgotten heroes in their respective fields as they attended to family needs and either prepared ahead for us or walked beside us during a challenging time in our history.

Here we attempt to condense our loved ones' lives by noting some of their best qualities. These short descriptions capture the essence of each life so that you will know our deep love for them as you follow along our grief journeys:

Anna Louise, known as Princess Girl
Born October 18, 1985
Died February 19, 2020
Age: 34

The essence of the life of Anna Louise is hard to put into words. Being in her presence was truly a gift. Those who shared her daily life and care provide us with a look into her short but remarkable life journey:

> Anna Louise had a strong will, undeniable attitude, and big presence that she channeled into a joyful life despite both physical and mental disabilities. Anna approached every day with bright eyes, a beaming smile, and an infectious laugh. When she wasn't with her family, she spent time with her friends at Imagine!, a day program for adults with special needs where she was nothing short of a celebrity among her caregivers and peers. She also loved (and was loved by) animals including her dogs, Lucy, Stanlee, and Buffy and her cat Clee.
>
> Anna had a deep love and passion for the arts. She was a gifted artist who used her work to give us a glimpse into her inner world. She also

loved listening to music all day, every day, especially anything with heavy drums.

(Written by Anna's brother, Benjamin, and published as her obituary)

Jeff, Ben, Anna Louise and Maureen

Next is from Anna's mom, Maureen.

Anna was objectively beautiful, with an angelic face, long, dark, silky hair worn in a bouncy ponytail and bangs framing the most incredible green eyes any of us have ever seen. Beyond her physical beauty, though, was her spirit; an aura, a radiance that surrounded her. She had a presence that commanded attention wherever she went. Anna was not to be ignored.

Anna had the power to bring out the goodness, the kindness in people. It could be anyone from the random stranger at the theme park who was moved to purchase and present her with a stuffed animal to friends who named their baby daughters after her to adoring staff at her day program who confided to me in secret that she was their favorite.

This tiny, delicate-appearing little girl, whose clinical presentation would suggest a life full of limitations, defied those expectations in every way. Anna had a personality that refused to be ignored. Her giggle was infectious. Holding hands with her was like a form of therapy. Taking her for walks with her faithful dogs or watching her swim were opportunities to observe moments of pure bliss. On the other hand, she also had the ability to bring people to their knees when she was not pleased. She could also be a little rascal, lying in her bed late at night, acting silly as the rest of the family pleaded with her to go to sleep.

Anna was my best friend, my soulmate, my confidante, my hero. She was her daddy's little princess. She was her brother's inspiration. She was exceptional in every way. She was love. She was light.

And now, Anna's Dad Jeff shares his reflection:

Anna was our first child, a beautiful young girl born in the mid-1980s to very young parents. We were so excited to bring her into the world. At birth she experienced a severe seizure disorder, which left us not knowing if she would survive the first week of her life. She was whisked away from her mother and taken for special observation and testing. All we could do was wait for the outcome. Although we were very young parents, my wife had a strong instinct about Anna and knew she would be okay.

In the first two years of her life, Anna suffered with neurological problems, but once again my wife persevered and pushed through for our daughter. I was clueless and kept thinking Anna would "outgrow" these obstacles and do all the things a child could do. She never did that. She never learned to ride a bike, she could not walk, she could not talk, she could not run and play, she could not go to a regular school.

Jeff and Anna Louise

Throughout her life we faced many challenges, from medical care to schools to simply sleeping well at night. Once again, my wife pushed through and provided Anna with the best life ever. She sacrificed a career and dedicated her entire life to our daughter.

A few years after Anna was born, we had a son, a bouncing baby boy with perfect health. He soon learned to love Anna as much as we did. I travelled a lot for my job, trying hard to provide for my family. My wife did all the heavy lifting with our children. She did a wonderful job!

Anna lived to be 34 years old, a beautiful young woman who could give back 1000 times more than what she could take in just by her presence in life. She was an incredible artist, and our home is filled with her work. We lost her unexpectedly, tragically, and in an instant, she was gone from our lives. In the end her body just gave out on her. We did everything we could to save her, but could not.

We struggle each day she is gone. It's difficult. We try to find a small shimmer of light and count the days until we can see her again. We do know her spirit is with us. We miss her every day, and our house is just too quiet and empty. We push through, the best we can. We learn to live with the unacceptable.

(Written by Anna's dad, Jeff)

Wade Edward, known as the Captain
Born June 4, 1943
Died July 18, 2020
Age: 77

Wade received considerable recognition and countless awards for his accomplishments and contributions in his professional career path, as a captain in the Michigan State Police, an attendee of the Federal Bureau of Investigation (FBI) Academy, and as fire marshal for the State of Michigan. Far beyond his commitment to his profession, his true joy was evident through the practice of his Catholic faith and the care and service to family and community. The following tributes are written by Wade's widow, Debra, and by his stepdaughters, Amber and Nora.

My husband Wade was an exceptional man, a supportive husband, a great stepdad and grandfather and a trusted friend to others. He wasn't big on words, but he was always there for us and for everyone. He was totally dedicated to the safety and well-being of people in general. He truly made you feel safe in his presence. He had your back and you knew it.

His training in his career field, which included 32 years of his life, gave him a sense of responsibility to others. He loved his profession, and he was always grateful to have served. He carried those values and the training into his personal life and relationships. What made him a great law enforcement officer was his core values in life, in particular his Catholic faith. He emulated Christ in his love for others through his protection and leadership skills gained.

Wade loved the outdoors and found it a peaceful place to reflect on life. He also had a love for planting and harvesting large vegetable gardens. This was more than a hobby for Wade. He loved planting and watching the food grow, and it was his additional way to help others as he shared the harvest with all.

Wade had a bit of a fun side when he twirled you on the dance floor to polka music. He enjoyed seeing the surprise on the faces of his dance partners. He always thought he could "wear out" my elderly aunts on the dance floor, but much to his surprise, they outlasted his attempts.

His true joy came from supporting our blended family. He was so involved in the lives of my daughters and their children, his stepgrandchildren. We miss his presence in all our special events where he had made wonderful efforts to support and encourage their young lives. We will always attribute a huge part of their accomplishments today to Wade's love, along with his direction and support, which was unwavering.

(Written by his widow, Debra)

Debra & Wade
June 7, 1997

The next tribute is from his stepdaughters.

When we first met our future stepdad Wade, we were of the age where young girls (ages 15 and 12 at the time) were not particularly fond of their mom dating someone with a police background. He seemed to be rigid, which was the total opposite of our mother. We saw right away that he thought he was the authority, but we thought we held that role. He came across as somewhat strict, but we were stubborn girls.

After he married our mother, we somehow learned, after many challenging attempts on both ends, to find common ground. One example that comes to mind is how much we struggled with his insistence on organization. He obsessed, in our view, over putting tools back into the exact same slot we had taken them from. Soon we realized that it wasn't so much about where he wanted his tools returned to; rather, he was trying to teach us to be responsible. We reluctantly went along with his requests. Wade, in our eyes, eventually came to the middle in terms of expectations for his new role as stepdad in our young lives.

Amber, Wade and Nora

Prior to marrying our mother, Wade had three adult children from his first marriage but was a busy provider, working long hours during their childhood. Two years after marrying our mother, he retired from his profession. We became his second opportunity to take on this father role. Even in our struggles as teenagers, we began to see beyond his strictness and learned to appreciate his efforts to make our blended family work. We felt loved and protected. What we saw next is that Wade had an exceptional understanding of being a parental figure, or stepgrandfather, in his 3rd time around with our children, his stepgrandchildren.

We ended up loving the fact that he did not give up on us; he was there for us through it all, and in the end we were there for him in his illness and dying. We cherish our memories of this selfless man, a strong force in our lives, a man our children called "Poppy."

(Written by his stepdaughters, Amber and Nora)

Anna Marie, known as Sparkle
Born October 2, 1928
Died October 26, 2020
Age: 92

My mother, Anna Marie, was a genuine and kind soul. She loved people, fashionable clothes, and pumpkin pie. Her piercing blue eyes truly sparkled. She was so devout in her Catholic faith that she prayed for all the religious and for their ministry before any of her own needs. She had a natural wisdom like no other human being I have ever met. She was my north star.

The words that best capture her spirit were written tributes, one posted to social media for the world to see just two days after her death and the other written and read at her eulogy for private mourners. They both exhibit the love she gave so freely and the gentle nature of her character.

Mom often had me show her my Facebook posts and was captivated with photos we would post of her on the social media platform. It seems fitting that I share what my son posted on October 28, 2020.

This week the world lost an amazing woman. She lived humbly and selflessly. She exuded love and peace and was a sparkling example of living a life of faith, hope, and love. She was hilarious, mostly not on purpose, but in an innocent and honest way. She was devoted to her faith, her husband, and her seven children. She suffered the loss no parent should have to endure, one of her beloved children, and she did so with the same sense of peace she held all her life.

I cannot adequately express in words how amazing she was. She brought me such joy, and in her presence, I always felt comfort. My worries would melt away in one conversation with her. I think her favorite phrase was "oh well" because she never let a single thing bother her. Rest in peace, Grandma. May God give you repose, and may your soul be welcomed into God's kingdom. I know they rolled out the red carpet for you. I love you. Jon

(Written by her grandson "Jonnie")

Anna Marie with grandson Jon

The next tribute is a reflection written by her youngest daughter Melissa, which she also delivered as Mom's eulogy on the eve of All Saints Day in 2020.

Anna Marie Elizabeth N.—A.M.E.N., Annie Sparkles, Irish Annie. She loved to talk. Always wanting to "visit," she drew you in with her ease and comfort. She was simple, genuine, loving, steady, calm and wise. She was fun and funny. She was strong. She was positive, hopeful, and a beacon of light.

Her relationships with people were the most important thing in her life, those with God, family, friends and even with complete strangers. She was the type of woman who loved and emulated Christ. Rooted deep in her Catholic Faith, it was the center of who she was. She never missed church and always found a way to bring God into any conversation.

She was the type of daughter who walked to church with her family—every Sunday until a neighbor stopped and offered them a ride. She was the type of daughter who, at 14, drove her mom to work and was pulled over by the police—only to talk her way out of it.

She was the type of sister who was more like a best friend. She couldn't wait to go "up home" as she called it, to be with her beloved sisters. She would shout out "Now entering Huron County!" as we passed the little green county sign entering into Kinde, Michigan. When she was with her sisters, it was laughing, music, reminiscing and nonstop talking into the wee hours of the night. They loved nothing more than just being together.

She was the type of wife who loved unconditionally, sacrificed, and honored her wedding vows. Her tenderness and love made my dad a better man. She often told of how she fell in love with him the very first time she saw him on the school bus. She would say "he had the prettiest blue eyes" and "it was his boots that made me fall for him!" She was the type of wife who took the money he sent home at wartime—that he had intended for her to save, and instead figured it was much more fun to take everyone to the movies, her treat!

She was the type of friend who made you a priority. She listened and laughed. She quickly made friends with the ladies from TOPS (Take Off Pounds Sensibly), church, and the entire neighborhood—from Magnolia Lane to Carr Road. Her house was the one that everyone wanted to be at. She could usually be found in the kitchen, barefoot, radio on, making a batch of her famous french fries. She took special care of the neighborhood children—loving them like her own. Those friendships, with both the children and their parents, lasted a lifetime.

She was the type of mom who read nursery rhymes, rocked you to sleep, named your dolls, made up funny songs and stories. She ran her hand through your hair when you were sick or tired. She was the type of mom who was your rock and your best friend. She often prescribed a warm washcloth to the forehead and a cup of hot tea cured every illness and solved any problem you could ever have.

She was the type of grandmother who took the time to go on walks with you and play with you; she would let you get away with pretty much anything. Like spinning on a swing until it made you sick, but then she would lay with you all night. If you wanted to run away, she would help you pack your bags, simply asking, "What are you going to do for money?"

Melissa Ann, Anna Marie and author Laurel

On this special day, as Mom gets promoted to Heaven, probably as the Angel in charge of dancing and Heavenly parties, let us remember that the hardest thing to erase is a mother's love. Mothers reflect God's love, and because of that, we should always honor our mother and return that love with our whole hearts. And honor her, we did.

May the road rise up to meet you—
May the wind always be at your back
May the sunshine warm upon your face,
The rains fall soft upon your fields and until we meet again,
May God hold you in the palm of His hand.
Fly high, Mom! We love you.
(Written by her daughter, Melissa Ann)

Mark Thomas, known as the Chief
Born November 3, 1958
Died November 24, 2020
Age: 62

Mark was an exceptional human being, one whom you encountered and whose words stayed with you long after your visit. The last time I saw him was in late August 2020. It was an unexpected and long conversation that will be cherished. Since I was passing by his home area, I was asked to meet up with him to pick up some items for the northern family hunting cabin. We met in a parking lot and had an outside visit because of the contagion. He was late arriving and apologized. Within minutes we were engaged in great conversation, as he always set you at ease. I remember coming home and saying to my husband, "That was such a nice encounter with your brother. We talked about so many joys and struggles and laughed together." I am grateful I have that memory. The following tributes were written first by his widow, Becky, and then by his brother, Kevin.

Mark was larger than life. His presence filled a room the minute he entered it. His smile and laughter would soon follow, which included his imitated voices accompanied by just about any sound you could ever imagine. He spent years mastering his art. Children were especially drawn to him and he to them.

Mark loved his family and friends and was extremely diligent in all his duties. In each role he was given in life, as a son, brother, cousin, friend, husband, uncle, father, stepfather, and grandpa (Pa), he triumphed in his efforts to show love.

He worked tirelessly to provide for his family, which included a newborn grandson arriving when Mark was 43 years old. Mark became the main father figure to Aaron who called him Dad for 12 years. He was exceptional in every way and took this dual role of father/grandfather very seriously. He said that God had given him a second chance to be a Father, and he was so grateful for the opportunity.

Mark had so much love to give and would always leave you with a big hug and a "love you." He loved large and laughed loud and hard, oftentimes to the point of tears. These tears flowed daily for him. He took nothing for granted and was not afraid to show his feelings.

Mark was an amazing and unique human being. He was loved by all who knew him. For our family, he was "The Chief," and we are forever grateful for his selfless love and for the incredible life he lived.

(Written by his beloved wife, Becky)

Mark Thomas with wife Becky and step-daughter Krystal

The next tribute is written by Kevin:

My only brother, Mark, was five years my junior and the youngest of four children. Never, ever did I entertain the thought that I would lose him, given our age difference. He was a great brother to me, and I enjoyed watching him as a devoted husband, father and grandfather. He was my best friend.

He was a natural-born entertainer. He loved to impersonate cartoon character voices and celebrities from childhood to adulthood. In his youth, sadly, he got offtrack for several years with an addiction. On New Year's Day 1991, he committed himself to rehabilitation and was very active in his Narcotics Anonymous group. He brought in many people to this great organization through the sharing of his own struggles. He was 30 years clean and sober at the time of his untimely death.

Mark loved the outdoors, especially hunting and fishing. His favorite fishing spot was at our family cabin in the Upper Peninsula of Michigan. His fishing skills were exceptional. He also enjoyed birdwatching. He and his youngest son spent much of their time together admiring, learning about, and feeding birds in the environment around their home.

He worked in the building trades and was an excellent carpenter. Finished carpentry work was his trademark. He taught Sunday school to children at his church and enjoyed sharing his faith with them. Like myself and our father, he was also a member of the local city fire department servicing the community for many years.

He had a unique ability with children that is hard to put into words, as you had to see him in action. His ability to light up their faces was unique. He would get down on the floor with them, and they would squeal with delight. His love for children was a gift. He impersonated Donald Duck to hear them howl with pleasure. All in all, he emulated Christ as a fisherman, carpenter, lover of children, teacher of the faith and all-around good man.

Early in his adult life he was diagnosed with non-Hodgkin's lymphoma, was successfully treated, and declared cancer-free. In early 2020, he discovered an enlarged lymph node along his jawline and was told his cancer had returned. He was treated and beat the cancer a second time, getting the good news from his oncologist in early fall of 2020. Sadly, a few days later, he was contacted and told that he had been exposed to Covid-19 in his doctor's office. He became ill, was Covid-19 positive and transported by ambulance on his 62nd birthday to the hospital. He died a few weeks later with no family at his side because of the contagion and no vaccines.

We had a great relationship, one that included much love. In the last ten years of his life, we had regular phone conversations as we lived an hour from each other. We never had a harsh word, ever. I am grateful that he was my brother, and I will miss him forever, until we meet again. (Note: a version of this was also spoken at the gravesite during interment).

(Written by Mark's brother, Kevin)

Kevin and Mark Thomas in the Upper Peninsula of Michigan

One last life story I would like to include is that of Blessed Michael McGivney. I knew very little about this wonderful young priest when I wrote this book, other than he was the founder of the Catholic fraternal order Knights of Columbus in 1882 for the purpose of spiritual support for Catholic men and financial resources for families who had suffered loss.

After becoming discouraged about the complexity and time involved in finding a publisher, I asked for his intercession during prayer time with my husband. We had attended a dinner that evening hosted by the Knights of Columbus council in our home parish for members and their spouses. We were encouraged to take a prayer card home with us to pray for the canonization of Blessed Michael McGivney into sainthood.

I felt a tinge of guilt asking for intercession when my need was not urgent or of a matter that would be considered miraculous. We, as Catholics, believe that in our prayer time, in addition to petitioning God, we can (and should) also call upon those who have gone before us marked with the sign of the faith, to pray for and with us. It is a comforting practice to ask others to join us in prayer, whether they are here on earth or have gone on to their eternal home. Although my need was out of the ordinary, my husband reassured me that prayer brings results and reminded me that we have witnessed this our entire lives.

The very next morning, I learned of Covenant Books Publishing. I reached out to another author who had published with them, and he was very pleased with the process and the final product. When I signed a contract to publish with them (two weeks later), I became quite curious to learn more about Fr. McGivney, as I felt there was an intercessory prayer answered. At this moment in our history when Catholic priests suffer stigma (and persecution) for the sins of the brotherhood related to the recent scandals in the Church, I wanted to recognize the contributions of our "good and faithful priests," which date back centuries.

I was in awe of what I learned about the life of this nineteenth-century man of God. There were too many parallels to ignore. He had a heart for the bereaved, in particular for the widowed and orphaned, and he advocated for their help. He triumphed over grief and let it transform him into action that brought help to others. Sadly, he died a young death, just two days after his thirty-eighth birthday, after falling ill during the flu pandemic of 1889.

Bl. Michael McGivney, known as the Good Samaritan
Born August 12, 1852
Died August 14, 1890

Portrait of Father McGivney by Chas Fagan
Credit: Knights of Columbus Multimedia Archives

Michael McGivney was born in 1852 to Irish immigrant parents, Patrick and Mary (Lynch) McGivney in Waterbury, Connecticut. He was the oldest of thirteen children, six of whom died in infancy or childhood. Grief was not a stranger to this family. His father died in 1873 when Michael was only twenty years old and attending seminary.

He began his priestly duties on Christmas Day in 1877 in New Haven. Fr. McGivney was beloved by his parishioners. Those who were closest to him noted they were impressed by his energy and intensity. He was there for the people in all circumstances.

In a famous case that had widespread news coverage, he attended to the needs of James "Chip" Smith, a twenty-one-year-old Catholic who ended up on death row after shooting and killing a police officer while he was intoxicated. It is written that Fr. McGivney offered prayer, comfort, and the Mass in the city's jail cell to this condemned man. These daily visits lasted months and had a profound effect on the prisoner. The media credited Fr. McGivney's visits to this young man's change in demeanor.

On execution day, after Mass, Fr. McGivney's grief was profound. The prisoner, Chip Smith, tried to console him by saying,

> Father, your saintly ministrations have enabled me to meet death without a tremor. Do not fear for me, I must not break down now. (A Model for Today, Fr. McGivney Guild)

The priest walked with the prisoner to the end, leading him in prayer and blessing him. Fr. McGivney organized a total abstinence society to fight alcoholism, letting his deep grief be transformed into action and help for others.

He was also relentless in his efforts to explore with the laity the idea of a Catholic, fraternal benefit society to strengthen religious faith and provide for the needs of bereaved families. In 1882 the legislature of the state of Connecticut granted a charter to the *Knights of Columbus* whose original core principles were "unity" and "charity" with "fraternity" and "patriotism" later added. Today, it is one of the largest Catholic organizations in the world with two million members across the globe.

In March 2008, Blessed McGivney was declared a Venerable Servant of God by Pope Benedict XVI and was beatified on the eve of All Saints Day, October 31, 2020. To learn more about the story of this exemplary American priest and his road to sainthood, see the Father Michael J. McGivney Guild.

PART I

Embracing Change

CHAPTER 1

Loss and Change

....

*Remember that when you leave this earth, you can take with you
nothing that you have received, only what you have given; a full
heart, enriched by honest service, love, sacrifice and courage.*
—St. Francis of Assisi

....

Working through bereavement is a giant undertaking and one
that is often thrown upon us. It is even more stressful when we are
unable to be with the dying as was the case for so many in the pandemic years. Additionally, it is very difficult to move through the
changes that accompany loss when the world in which we live is so
uncertain. Our stress levels and coping mechanisms are impacted by
the times in which we live. Unfortunately, we are experiencing an
overload in our mental health system for services, as the needs are
enormous on many fronts. The bereaved need our help and direction
to ease their feelings of sadness and loss during a time in our lives
when the world seems unpredictable.

There are many similarities in today's world to that of the times
when my first loss occurred, early on in my life some fifty years ago.
Although there was no pandemic, the world felt scary and out of
control. I start here with my first significant loss, which in part, con-

tributed to my interests in studying and helping bereaved individuals and families.

Heartbreaking loss arrives early

A very long time ago, in my junior year of high school, I participated in a cooperative educational program in the school office, where I was tasked with helping staff with errands, filing, and other office duties. I had joined the Business Leaders of America student group, and I wanted to gain some work experience. It was my desire to earn a recommendation letter for future work.

I knew the road to college looked bleak for me, as there were little resources to go around and little to no direction or advising. My parents saw graduation from high school as an accomplishment and encouraged finding a good man to settle down with and have a family. Additionally, opportunities for attaining a higher education were less encouraged for females by some at the time, in the late 1960s and early 1970s. If females did get good direction and a chance to attend college, it was viewed by many as a chance to find "Mr. Right" or the husband of their dreams. It was a long-standing joke to obtain the degree of MRS (or "Mrs. so-and-so").

Through this co-op experience, I met a kindhearted, soft-spoken man, the vice principal, Mr. Paul Cabell. Although he was a busy professional, he always made time to see how I was doing each day. Oftentimes, he would poke his head around the doorway of the little office space I was assigned to work in, and he would catch me by surprise. His smile was wide and his eyes welcoming to whoever was in his view. He had a special way of making one feel as though he had all the time in the world when you were in his presence. He was a genuine soul.

As the new year approached, 1972, the world conditions were worsening. Americans were dealing with numerous stressors in society. There was a continued fight for equality for marginalized groups, the beginning of an environmental movement, and the Vietnam War and the Anti-War Movement with protests. There was also a "New

Right" mobilizing in defense of political conservatism and traditional family roles.

Riots erupted between racial groups in our school hallways as students reacted to troubling times. There was continued racial tension and a great divide among the student body (65 percent White, 30 percent Black, 5 percent Hispanic/Latino), causing enormous stress for Mr. Cabell in his administrative role. Fighting and beatings were becoming the norm in school hallways and in the neighborhood with out-of-control teenagers. This environment was especially troubling for me, as I had attended parochial schools in the elementary years where the emphasis was on peace, kindness, and inclusion of others, especially those considered on the margins of society.

Mr. Cabell, who identified as biracial, was known as a problem solver, and yet, in this situation, everything he tried with the students and with the administration seemed to fail from his perspective. The Whites felt he sided with the Black students, and the Black students thought he "acted too White." I remember seeing the agony on his face day after day and noticing how his infectious smile had disappeared over a few weeks' time. On an early morning in late February, after writing a three-page letter to the student body and one to his young wife of three years, this twenty-six-year-old accomplished professional shot and killed himself in his home.

> I die to emphasize to you and all minority
> people who ever dream to be free that it can only
> come through working together.

These were the words of Mr. Cabell, which he wrote to his students before he took his own life. He continued,

> It seems that there is no other way for me to
> get your attention.

The news of his death shattered us. The aftermath was, at times, unbearable, yet together we muddled our way through it, without much help from the adults. It was a loss that changed my life as I witnessed deep psychological pain in so many of my friends (of all colors) and the school office staff, yet there were very few strategies for healthy coping skills realized or shared. In some respects, our grief was policed and regulated. We were expected to "move on" without questioning the enormous disruptive event of the death of a man we had known and whose kindness radiated the hallways of our school.

At my young age, I had not experienced any significant loss other than a paternal grandmother and our family pet. I was as lost as the others but intuitive as I processed the grief and watched my peers and their unattended suffering. I desired to do something, anything to ease the pain.

I remember asking myself, What would Mr. Cabell want me to do? I struggled with the loss of such a kind man and recognized that he deserved a better legacy than his desperate last attempt. I knew instinctively he would want me to show genuine care for others as he had shown for all people. Even though I was not schooled in loss at that early age, I seemed to know how to be silently present for others as they talked about their guilt, shame, and regret along with the change this tragedy brought into our young lives.

With the help of a loving faith-filled mother, I accepted that his suicide was a very complex death and loss to experience and process. Even with a letter of explanation, there would be questions that would never be answered. I developed a strong belief in my capacity to help ease the suffering of others, in particular those who are bereaved. As my life moved on, I gained more tools and strategies that equipped me to understand and work through loss in a healthy way. For a time, I worked as a paralegal in a law office where the attorneys specialized in Probate, Wills, and Estates. In that capacity, I met the bereaved as well. Eventually, I expanded those skills through my educational pursuit, later in my life, to study and research the sociology of grief and bereavement.

A sociological view

It is important to note how I view the experiences of grief and loss as natural human events that need *to be lived through*, and not ones that need healing or recovery. As a symbolic interactionist,[1] I believe that these common terms used (in the media, in support groups, etc.) can medicalize our experience of grief. When you lose someone whom you love, you are not sick or in need of recovery. You might feel empty and/or broken or as if a big part of you is missing; however, healing and recovery are more suitable terms for illness and accidents. We must ask ourselves, What are we recovering from? What needs healing? Loss and change are experiences in life we will all encounter, which need to be processed or lived through. And this is why when we are stricken with grief, support from compassionate others who understand loss is essential.

I resonate with the work of Arthur Frank in *The Wounded Storyteller*, a great read and one I have assigned to students in health courses. This work and my experience of bereavement fits the "quest narrative" that Frank identifies as one in "which the long and painful journey of grief can become a pilgrimage of personal growth and development" (Frank 1995 and Walter 2001, p. 192). It involves a transformational phase instead of a speedy return to the status quo.

Tony Walter's work is relied upon heavily in my search to understand how our society influences our grief and mourning. Through his work as a British sociologist, he points to the cultural norms in place, which dictate how we should feel and behave and their impact on people. He thoroughly examines the regulation of emotions (policing of grief) in his seminal work *On Bereavement: The Culture of Grief*, which I lean on in my coursework for students.

Sociologist Peter Marris reminds us that "the fundamental crisis of bereavement arises, not from the loss of others but from the loss of self" (P. Marris 1974, 2014). We may feel as though we have lost a part of who we are (in relationship to the deceased). The person we loved who has died can no longer return the love in the relationship we always had with them. In large part, therefore, grief from a significant loss can be debilitating, and the self becomes fractured.

---

[1] When applying social interactionist theory, social scientists observe patterns of interaction between individuals. This includes the use of symbols, such as language, which has the potential to shape our experiences.

Structures of meaning need reconstructing. Significant loss has the potential to impact our entire being, the physical, social, psychological, emotional, and spiritual realms.

I remember a research participant many years ago comparing her grief process as a new widow to that of what a lower limb amputee must feel like in the beginning of their loss and adjustment. Suddenly, a large part of you is missing. You must learn how to be in the world all over again. You need crutches and help. She noted that the world seemed hard to maneuver as a widow, but with her crutches (the support group), she just might learn this new and challenging landscape. Everything seemed different, and the grief was exhausting. Her sense of self was impacted.

Marris wrote widely on the topics of loss, change, and bereavement in many contexts and showed the importance of understanding grief. He suggests that by doing so, it can help us to comprehend processes of all types of change (both personal and social). He encouraged us to have more compassion for ourselves and others in dire circumstances as we restore the structures of meaning in our lives after loss. He saw similar parallels of these fractured structures whether from a loss of a personal relationship or other predictable social context of an interpretable world. As we have witnessed in these past few years, as a society, we fell into a condition of anomie or normlessness—a concept coined by an early sociologist Emile Durkheim. The pandemic haze changed our daily routines and customs, yet new norms took a great deal of time to develop as we learned about the contagion. For those of us grieving new losses, we lost traditional support as well and had to help ourselves for the most part.

The outcome and time frame for moving through the grief in a healthy fashion are dependent on numerous factors. This includes the type of relationship, the mode of death, the support one has, and so much more. It is often an agonizing and long journey of mixed emotions to process. It is not a series of stages that are linear in nature, such as those promoted by the media.[2]

---

[2] The famous five-stage loss theory popularized mostly by the media—denial, anger, bargaining, depression, and finally, acceptance (DABDA)—has been

Today, with the backdrop of an uncertain and chaotic world, bereaved individuals appear to be experiencing an "altered grief" because of the limitations and restrictions from a contagious virus that were part of our initial circumstances in 2020 and 2021. In some instances, people we loved died alone. Those who are left behind, the families and medical professionals, still grapple with the restrictions that were in place in the initial phase of the pandemic, both at the bedside and for the inability to have proper rituals both during the dying and afterward to honor the deceased.

Many of us struggle with a feeling of having our grief disenfranchised as the deaths of our loved ones from COVID-19 seem trivialized. It could be helpful to the millions of mourners to have a national or global day of remembrance to honor those who died of COVID-19. Perhaps because the deaths continue and the pandemic is still unfolding, we have yet to have collective mourning. We have had messages about how "we are all in this together"; however, those who have lost someone as a direct result of the contagion do not see it that way. Yes, we all had to go into survival mode, but not all of us lost a close other. Many moved on with life without a major loss to process.

Some of the coronavirus victims were honored by local and national media, but those few highlighted were a fraction of the loss stories. Families who were closely impacted have noted that our collective losses have not been well-memorialized. I do believe that this lack of recognition has contributed to more pain in an altered grief landscape. When the mode of death of your loved one is "top of the news" repeatedly for long periods of time, it can feel as though the person you lost is a statistic and that their death is being diminished. This, too, is hard to process. Everywhere we went, it seemed people were talking about COVID-19 deaths as if they were to be expected.

After the September 11, 2001, attack, the *New York Times* published in their "Nation Challenged" section a series of scaled-down

---

mistakenly applied to the experience of bereavement. The stages, as set forth by Elizabeth Kubler-Ross, were originally intended to be observations of those who were dying.

profiles of people who died in the World Trade Center tragedy. They entitled this work "Portraits of Grief." It was one of their most commented on works by their readers. It would be a major undertaking to compile all the deaths to date from COVID-19 and, in part, a real challenge because of the way in which some deaths were reported (and unreported). However, I think that some type of tribute to not only those we lost but to the scores of first and last responders who were by their sides would be a tremendous testament to the lives lost and to the heroes suffering today, who are leaving their professions in record numbers.

There was also an amazing collection of the 9/11 portraits of grief published in book form by *Times Books,* highlighting the unique and precious lives of those lost in the tragedy. Our collective grief from COVID-19 has not been adequately recognized, and people are left wondering if we really were/are "in this together." Countless people have spoken to me about how to process the grief on both the collective and personal levels.

I am often asked if I can steer people in the direction of a guideline to help with their personal grief so that they can "do it right." I wish it were that simple. Working through grief is messy and varies widely. Anna Bardsley, in *Fluttering on Fences: Stories of Loss and Change* (I. Renzenbrink 2010) gives us her view:

> I have heard grief described as a "process," heard the words, "stages of grief." Process and stages are such tidy words and grief is anything but tidy or orderly; it is a mess, much more like a storm raging outside my window. A storm which buffets me at its will. Winds that rage, then subside, only to rage again. Rain that drenches me or drizzles and drizzles until I am wet through. Sometimes I can hold up an umbrella and take shelter. Other times there is no shelter, the umbrella is torn and ripped out of my hands. I am left alone and vulnerable to the power of the storm raging around and within me.

Regardless of how we define our loss or what we call this experience during our lifetimes, whether that be a process, a journey, a storm, or a new chapter, these deaths and the grief that follows change our narratives. We find ourselves grieving "what was and what could have been."

The good news is that research shows, and personal experience indicates, that with ample support, most bereaved individuals will learn to adapt to the loss in a healthy fashion. In addition to personal support, we also can benefit from today's wide array of resources available in many formats. This help may come through books, support groups, art therapy, poems, or simply the quiet presence of a kind other to witness our pain. Support persons, from family and close friends and oftentimes complete strangers in support groups, become critical in helping us to feel that we are not alone in our circumstances. They help us to construct our new narrative due to the loss.

There are many incidences, however, that can derail our grief as Dr. Kathleen Shear, the founding director of the Center for Complicated Grief at Columbia School of Social Work has put forth in her research. Dr. Shear points out that anything that gets in the way of accepting the reality of the death or one's inability to see the future in a positive way both have the potential to disrupt a healthy adaptation in the grief process.

Our grief stories from a COVID-19 death often fit these categories. We may have, for a time, wanted to blame someone for the COVID-19 death; after all, the deceased family member would still be with us had it not been for the mishandling of the pandemic. This is what Dr. Shear notes may fit a counterfactual scenario that can derail our grief. It was okay to think about it in those terms, but we had to then pull back and adjust to the reality. We could not change the circumstances, and there were many complex factors involved in the mishandling of the pandemic. There was no one person or entity to blame.

Dr. Shear also suggests that part of a healthy adaptation to loss includes not only accepting the reality of the loss, but in addition, we need to adjust to the secondary losses that often accompany them.

We also need to accept a different type of relationship or connection with the one who died. She stresses the need to be able to see a future with some promise and to reconnect with others to find meaning in our lives.

It has been a long and arduous road for many families who have lost someone during the pandemic years, especially if the death was a direct result of the virus. As Marris reminded us; we lost a part of ourselves with those who died. And with current world conditions, it is sometimes very difficult to see the future in a positive way. We have lost our sense of safety in the world, which is what sociologist Anthony Giddens calls ontological security, which incorporates a belief in the trustworthiness of our surroundings and the ability to continue our own life stories within them. This should provide us with the capacity to keep these stories going. But during the pandemic, it took great courage and perseverance to embrace the changes in our lives while carrying grief. Through the collecting of our stories and sharing them widely, we hope to inspire others to find their courage. As with any story, there is a beginning, and so we start with the news of the 2020 deaths in our own families.

Key takeaways

> Examine your first loss for insight.
> Cultural norms influence our grief.
> Loss is an experience, not an illness.
> Utilize a wide array of resources.
> Embrace change with perseverance.
> Identify or create strong support.

C H A P T E R   2

The News

....

Bad news is bearable with the right people
beside you on the journey.

—Anonymous

....

The year 2020 brought so much bad news to our family that my writing of this book was delayed. A feeling of being grief-stricken took hold. After the first significant loss in the early months of 2020, I didn't want to be overcome with deep sorrow and anguish, yet I was. I wanted to remain calm, fully present and composed in order to support those most impacted in the family. I wanted to encourage them to journal because I feared that without traditional support, the grief would become complicated.

I suggested they write down what helped and what hindered their grief. I had hope that by capturing our grief in my writing (and theirs), others in similar circumstances would also be helped by whatever strategies worked for us. I also knew the value of constructing the story, and with lockdown, our ability to do so in a traditional way with others was nearly impossible.

We kept getting knocked down in 2020 with more bad news, coupled with unexpected family dysfunction, and attempts at writing stalled for all of us. With so much ongoing high emotion, I realized we could not write.

As time moved on, in relation to the impact of isolation and restrictions during the pandemic, I began to hear more stories of unresolved loss from my students and from the general public (through news broadcasts, my online teaching, and in research). After witnessing the agony of altered grief in my own family, and hearing about it from others, I knew I had to push through and begin to tell our stories.

The unwelcome death call

Getting bad news, such as the death of a family member or close other, can be (and was for us) distressing. The unwelcome bad news has the potential to cause shock, disbelief, and complete numbness. Some people have even collapsed upon the news of a death. I have had people tell me that they felt a shock wave go through their entire body. There is even a rare, temporary heart condition known as broken heart syndrome (stress cardiomyopathy), which can be brought on because of the amount of stress hormone released in the body upon bad news. Communicating a death to others should be done thoughtfully and gently, preferably in person and with great compassion.

News of my niece Anna Louise's death came suddenly in mid-February 2020, just before the entire world was about to change. We received a phone call from Colorado. I was sitting with my ninety-one-year-old mother, in her living room. We were viewing a television news broadcast where we were engaged in friendly banter as we watched the circus of political candidate commercials when the phone call came in. If it had not been for caller ID, I would have never recognized the agonizing screams on the other end of the call. "She's gone, she's gone, our little girl is gone."

I quietly listened to the hysterical crying and breathlessness of the voice on the other end. A part of me went numb, but at the same time, I knew I must stay focused and help this devastated mom, someone whom I love dearly. I used my sister-in-law's name, Maureen, and asked her where she was and who was with her. She gathered herself a bit to tell me she was at the hospital and that my brother was there somewhere too along with my nephew, their adult son, and his girlfriend (now wife). I knew not to ask too many questions given her state of mind. She wailed again in agony, and it broke me.

Mom remained quiet yet concerned as she waited for the call to end. Obviously, she knew by the look on my face and my pacing of the condo first floor that this news was not good. She had muted the television and sat gripping the remote control tightly. It was the hardest news I had ever been summoned to give her. Her granddaughter Anna Louise had died suddenly in the emergency room being prepped for unforeseen surgery.

Mom went silent, no questions, no tears, only a blank stare ahead as she quietly said, "Oh no, oh no." We shut the television off and gazed vacantly into a silent living room for a very long time. My niece was not only Mom's granddaughter but her namesake as well. I began to make calls to be sure the immediate family knew, and most had been notified and reacted in much the same way.

Mom and I finally prayed together and waited for the next call to come in. That is all we could do. We both felt paralyzed for hours. We had no particulars and did not feel it was appropriate at the time of the phone call to ask what happened but could only imagine what they had experienced and the devastation they must be feeling.

In preparing her excerpts for this book, Maureen recalls her 1985 feelings as a young first-time mother when she gave birth to her daughter, Anna, and how what should have been joyous news to share, by our culture's standards, became heartbreaking.

> I watched with joy and wonder as my daughter took her first breath. Joy and wonder that turned to fear and confusion as it became apparent that her brain and body were betraying her. I resigned myself to the fact that I would not have her for very long, that my fierce love would not save her. But I had underestimated this tiny girl. Clinically she had profound cognitive and

physical disabilities. But those labels are not indicative of the person I knew and raised. The child who even by objective standards was beautiful, with silky dark hair, the most striking green eyes and eyelashes so long they touched her eyelids, with a dazzling smile…the child who, as she grew up, had a charisma and a power to touch the lives of others that was in inverse proportion to her size. We named her Anna Louise after her two grandmothers. She lived 34 years, dying in February of 2020.

Anna Louise, aged three with Mom Maureen

When expected good news goes bad, emotions clash wildly. In this young mother's life, at the birth of her firstborn, there was a rejoicing of sorts, and yet there was fear that the worst was yet to come. What should have been a joyous event brought great uncertainty and helplessness and had the feeling of being a "mixed blessing." Prognosis was bleak. Little did any of us know, however, that this small, beautiful child would be a miracle on this earth for over three decades.

Anna's mom, Maureen, then recalls the details of her daughter's death that are remembered precisely as they happened.

My first experience with loss and grief was at the age of fifteen when my father died. In the many years since, I have attended the funerals of my mother, other beloved family members, friends and acquaintances. I had never witnessed a person die. I watched my daughter die. In a literal blink of an eye. I remember screaming at the ER nurse. I remember the call of Code Blue. I remember the room filling up with medical professionals. I remember the cardio-pulmonary resuscitation attempts. I remember a nurse explaining what was going on even as I knew lifesaving measures were ultimately futile. I remember begging my daughter not to leave me. I remember screaming that I needed her. "Please don't leave me. I need you." Over and over. I remember the aftermath. The shock. The confusion. The fury. The pleading with God to give her back to me. And it all unfolded like an episode of a television show. I was there, but I was also watching it from a disjointed, surreal place.

Our lives and that of our family changed in an instant. As noted, this was mid-February, and while our private lives were shaken, we had no idea what was unfolding for the entire planet, a global pandemic. Once that news was absorbed in mid-March of 2020, the immediate and abrupt changes to our lives and routines made it nearly impossible to initially process the memories of Anna. They were on hold as our grief was altered and the focus shifted to our own safety, our own mortality and that of close others.

Mixed blessings

At other times, the news of the death of someone loved can be somewhat of a mixed blessing, a welcome relief, a liberating loss. The witnessing of long-suffering for a loved one who was quite independent, husband Wade, coupled with the exhaustive caregiving of a close family member, cousin Debra, can often seem cruel. Such was the journey for my maternal cousin as she cared for her husband for many years with Lewy body dementia.

Just a few months after our niece's untimely death, and knee deep into the pandemic, in midsummer 2020, cousin Wade began to quickly fail. However, he had rallied before, so this was an ambiguous illness and loss to process and witness. As Dr. Pauline Boss notes in her work, people dealing with "ambiguous losses" fluctuate between hope and hopelessness on a regular basis.

It was July 2020, and we had watched a spectacular sunset together on the beach in one of Wade's favorite places in the thumb area of Michigan, not far from his cottage. But it was not without incident. Due to physical balance issues in his advanced dementia, Wade had stumbled down the beach and tumbled in, falling on the soft sand. We were used to it. We just assisted him and normalized the awkwardness. Shortly thereafter, we hugged, said our goodbyes, and parted. Two weeks later, he was gone. The news, although very sad, was not devastating at the time; rather, it was liberating in a sense for some, at least initially. His struggles, and that of his close caregivers, were over.

The death had been expected at some point in the near future, although one that was hard to envision, as there is great variation in dying for dementia patients. Wade had been active, alert, and mobile right up until a week before his death. His illness ebbed and flowed. We watched as he would be completely lucid one day to then suddenly not knowing who we were the next day or understanding a simple process that he had always known before. On that level, it was hard to absorb the news.

Delivering the news

Receiving bad news and giving it to others are both often undesirable events in our lives but ones to be expected. When our mother began to show signs of decline in early fall 2020 because of natural aging shortly after cousin Wade died, I prepared my heart.

I am fully aware of the concept of "anticipatory grief," where one experiences a feeling of impending loss occurring before a death. It seemed hard to grasp as I continued to care for her alongside the help from many siblings. I don't think you can completely *antici-pate* feelings and emotions until the person actually dies. Losing your mom, your best friend, and the matriarch of the family is never easy, regardless of how long you have had her. Adjusting to a previously held life role before the caregiving chapter began takes work, and it requires patience as you learn to develop new routines.

"Bereavement is the most unarguable, and at its most severe, the most ill-prepared of all the adjustments to loss with which we are commonly faced" (P. Marris 1974). Again, the remarkable work of sociologist Peter Marris in his seminal book *Loss and Change* helped me understand that even in the face of a life-limiting illness that has been noted as terminal, we often postpone the "work of grief" until our fears are confirmed and the person has actually died. We may anticipate the aftermath and even rehearse parts of it, but we cannot grasp the reality until we are in it. We only begin to come to terms with death once it has occurred.

As a death and grief educator for years, I was acutely aware of how to make death in the home as peaceful and natural as birth. Making calls, however, about a person's impending death and having to say to your sibling or adult child "it won't be long...so if you want to come and say goodbye, it's time" are as gut-wrenching as having to say "she's gone." I don't think we could have ever prepared our hearts for the void caused by losing our mom, grandmother, and friend. Family members and close friends were awaiting the news and expecting mom's passing. Brother Jeff remembers:

> There was a great sadness when the news came, as I knew I now would never hear her voice again, see her smile, hear her laugh; it's all gone in an instant and leaves a void. Although it's inevitable, it's not a calming sense.

19

This loss for Jeff was especially hard as he had also lost his daughter, Anna, just months earlier, yet in some ways, it was soothing. He was very close to his mother, and she was a big support for him throughout his life. At the same time, he also felt as though now, his mother and daughter were together as his faith teaches. It seemed a mixed blessing of sorts.

Our two Anna's

Disheartening update

Then there are those times when a crisis is unfolding, and we push aside the fact that bad news could come at any moment, even though the circumstances look bleak. Somehow, for the next round of bad news, we just stayed positive. It could be labeled "denial," but we saw our responses at the time as holding onto *reasonable hope*. We could not give up. We were storming heaven for help and on hold from the world around us.

Just weeks after we lost Mom, a family member was hospitalized with COVID-19. The immediate family communicated through texts and phone calls as "being there" was restricted. We did not allow pessimism in our communications. Mark had beat cancer. He was a fighter. He overcame major obstacles in his life. He can, and will, pull through this, we told each other. Prayer and reasonable hope sustained us, but the bad news came again, all too soon.

This death call notification was coming from an out-of-state sister by phone. It was unwelcome news about my husband's only brother Mark who was gone at age sixty-two from COVID-19 complications. Silence filled our environment. Shock. Disbelief. Sadness. Emptiness. This news, too, was disheartening and unexpected as was our niece's untimely death. We were not prepared for either of them. Unlike our very ill cousin Wade and our aged mother Anna, this death news hit us at our core being. Mark had just beat cancer and had so much life left to live.

The multiple ways in which the news of the death is communicated has been shown to impact bereavement in terms of how the grief is worked through initially. When given within the family, this is often done by phone and when possible, in person. Often people are immediately cognitively challenged, even when the death is expected. People need time to process the news, so making oneself available is important to answer forthcoming concerns and questions.

When delivered by a medical professional, more often in person than not, the importance of being self-aware of one's verbal and non-verbal communication is necessary when delivering this death news. One needs to be honest, sensitive, and patient as the receiver begins to grasp the reality. A sincere gaze showing empathy is needed. Writing out on paper the "next steps" to send home with the mourner is critical and often appreciated when news is given in person. In those initial moments for the newly bereaved family and/or individual, it is hard to know exactly what to ask.

In the work I have done with bereaved family members, I have often witnessed a great deal of anger projected toward "insensitive medical professionals" about how they communicated the bad news of the death. However, when one's bereavement begins with a sense of compassion from a family member or from the medical community, it is greatly valued. This approach also tends to be imitated from one family member to the next as they communicate the news and details to others.

Research studies continue to show the lasting impact from the way in which the death news is given to people and the influence it has on the recipient. In a medical setting, it has been noted that "the surviving family will never forget this moment, and will often recall the exact events of that day years later, including the manner in which the news was delivered" (Bogle and Go 2015).

I learned early on in my life that having (and following) a protocol for how to compassionately give the news of a family death is an important element. This is more relevant for medical professionals but is also applicable for the general public to consider. First, one must assess how much the relative knows about the situation, then avoid giving that news over the telephone when possible. Next, before giving details, ask the person how much they want to know, as sometimes it is all they can process at the time to just know that someone they loved is gone. Be sure to provide honest and accurate information that you have if they do want details. Offer support and respond to their initial feelings with empathy. This involves good listening skills and, when in person, an awareness of your nonverbal communication as noted earlier by a non-anxious silent presence to represent sincere empathy.

Occasionally, we learn about a death from social media. This format is not ideal, but in some instances, it can reach a large amount of people, so they have time to prepare for upcoming arrangements. Giving commiserations online after learning of the news of a death is another challenge, where most are conflicted. "Liking" the announcement on a Facebook page, for example, is ambiguous. "Sorry about your loss" in written (or spoken) word gets old. These online condolences are not meant to be substitutes for the in-person support. People in these initial bereavement circumstances often need so much more.

Other forms of electronic news of death, such as texting, are not optimal unless one chooses to text "please call me," and a phone conversation ensues. Honoring differences includes a respect for how the other may hear/see the news about the death and eventually how we can help each other by our support for the disruption that follows. We should never make assumptions here.

I would be remiss not to note that there are those who receive bad news and have no one to share it with. There is no one to pass it on to and get acknowledgment for their loss of this person and for the grief they are experiencing. Perhaps this is because of the age of the recipient whose circle of close others is smaller. Or it can be as a result of one's geographic location, for example, when there is no one around you who knew the deceased person, and so you are left holding all the pain.

The inability to be able to tell others that someone you cared for has died, and construct some sense of reality, is hard to accept for some mourners. The news of death is a vital starting point for these stories of loss as they are constructed.

The news of any death, expected or sudden, can shatter us, create a sense of disorientation, disbelief, cognitive fog, and an uprising of high emotion. The news may freeze us up as we attempt to absorb it all. We may be stunned and in disarray.

If you are the recipient of the bad news, know who you can count on and trust to guide you in making funeral arrangements or decisions, either on your behalf or right alongside assisting you. Contact them without hesitation or ask the person giving you the news to do so. To identify your best support persons, ask yourself now who has always had your back, in good times and bad? Who will know what to do? Who knows your values and can help with these difficult decisions? Oprah Winfrey's quote is a good reminder to us.

> Lots of people want to ride with you in the limo, but what you want is someone who will take the bus with you when the limo breaks down.

In other words, we should desire for good people to journey alongside us who will ride every wave, regardless of the circumstances. Ideally, we should find them and set them up ahead of time before a tragedy strikes.

If you are the giver of bad news, explore how you can support the person who has just experienced the loss. Follow their lead.

Listen to their concerns and honor them. Think outside of the box for them, as they are most likely in a cognitive fog and need help in the immediate aftermath when professionals, such as those in hospitals and nursing homes as well as funeral homes, will need decisions made quickly. Make calls for them to others if they are ready to make the death known. And most importantly, witness their pain as they process this news, with your quiet presence. Providing people with immediate support has the potential to soften the disruption that follows soon after a death.

A great resource on this topic of delivering the news of death can be found in the work of Lord and Stewart (2008) in their practical guide to death notification, *I'll Never Forget Those Words*. They remind the notifier that it is important to understand that it is natural for "a vastly wide range of emotional reactions" to occur. These include how

> some people will react with a primitive reaction, much like that of a frightened animal. Those whose basic reaction to stress is to become aggressive may curse, blame the notifier, or hit someone or something. Those whose basic reaction to stress is to flee may retreat to another room, run outside, or faint. Some may become behaviorally frozen. They may simply stare wide-eyed, incapable of doing or saying anything. Some may begin immediately to cry, moan, or wail. (p. 66)

Upon the news of death, eventually, after the shock and any memorial services in the immediate aftermath, each of us begins to work through the grief in our unique ways. This often involves moving through the memories we made with the deceased and looking at those memories we are unable to make going forward (what could have been). It may involve examining our new role/s in the family and reconstructing an identity without that person beside us in life. Good support in this period of disruption is crucial, both real and perceived. It is especially important to have support persons who knew the deceased and can help us move through the memories, both past and the unmade memories in the future, and who understand the nature of grief.

People remember details surrounding big events in their lives, in happy times, such as a wedding or birth of a child, and in tragic times as we discuss here from the death of someone loved. Typically, this attention to detail results because of the magnitude of emotion surrounding the event. Whether that news is from the joy and awe of a happy occasion or the devastation from tragedy, we remember.

Once this unwelcome news is given or received, one rule to remember is that "the worst bit is not the death—although it might feel at the time as if it is" (Nicholson 2006, p. 6). According to this author, "The first rule [of grieving] is that it takes far, far longer than you think," hence the need for strong support and self-compassion as the grief unfolds.

Sadly, bereaved individuals often tell me that just weeks after a funeral, most people, even close relatives, stop checking in on them. This leads to isolation and loneliness in one's initial part of bereavement. In some cases, it can cause an unhealthy, premature emptiness for those left behind. In the pandemic years, there was a forced isolation that resulted in loneliness, not only in the initial bereavement but also as time moved on, and people forgot about our losses.

The focus in this chapter has been on the various ways in which the news of a death is communicated and its impact on the mourner in terms of how they will begin to construct the story of loss. This often includes words used, the means for delivery (i.e., in person, phone call), who gave the news and whether it was compassionately done. These are important factors that often play a large part for the construction of the grief story ahead. When it is the news of an unexpected death, it often parallels a trauma response, which is another reason the details are vivid and memorable. Every piece becomes part of the opening story bereaved people begin to put together to find meaning in these difficult circumstances.

We need sensitivity and compassion when we share the news of a death and the circumstances surrounding it. There is great potential to crush people's hearts if the news is not given empathetically. It can easily be misinterpreted by the receiver and cause so much unnecessary suffering, which adds to the disruption that death brings.

Key takeaways for receiving bad news

> Remain seated and focus on breathing.
> Express emotions as they present.
> Identify support persons.
> Ask for help and next steps.

Key takeaways for giving bad news

> Give the news in person, if possible.
> Develop self-awareness of verbal and nonverbal communication.
> Be honest, sensitive, and patient.
> Show empathy and compassion.
> Assess how much the person knows and wants to know.
> Provide accurate information.
> Witness pain with your quiet, non-anxious presence.
> Offer support and next steps (written out).

CHAPTER 3

The Disruption

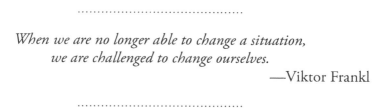

When we are no longer able to change a situation,
we are challenged to change ourselves.

—Viktor Frankl

The amount of disruption caused by the news of a death cannot be understated. We have heard the expression of how "life can change on a dime" meaning a rapid change in our circumstances that brings disruption, either good or bad. In the case of death, one's life is interrupted and sometimes changed forever, depending on the degree of the relationship, the age of the deceased, and the circumstances of the death.

The routines of daily living change immediately, especially if caregiving was a large part of everyday life. People feel dazed and sometimes are unable to function. Very few newly bereaved people take charge and spring into action. Death often causes a sense of chaos initially, and most mourners do not know what they are supposed to do next. This disruption is normal and common and why social support and ritual in the initial circumstances are important considerations for the newly bereaved.

The importance of initial support

I remember getting a call the day after my niece died suddenly. My brother and his wife were both on the call. It was no surprise to hear "we are not sure what to do and thought you could help." By helping the newly bereaved recall their lifelong values, we can assist these chief mourners to make the arrangements needed. Our help eases their burden. They both knew what to do once I reminded them of their values. But in the disruption and shock initially, it is challenging. These death arrangements, what to do with the body, where to have a service and when, often weigh heavy on the minds of those who must step up to make them at a time when they are cognitively depleted in their initial grief. Quick decisions must be made, and people need help, especially considering a sudden and unexpected death.

When I asked my brother when he wanted us to fly out to Colorado, his response was "Now, we need you now." The disruption was seemingly unbearable alone. His wife, Maureen, describes here what the outpouring of support meant to her in the initial grief period and the importance of presence and support through sharing in ritual just days after their daughter died:

> Supporting a grieving person is a challenging process. Every person has their own highly individual experience, so I feel qualified only to share my experience. I was overwhelmed by the number of people who came to my daughter's memorial service. It was a hastily arranged event, but we had friends and family travel from literally all four corners of the United States to attend. I was in a state of shock but was deeply moved by the outpouring of love and generosity we received from close family, friends and even casual acquaintances. We were surrounded by a community of people united by a shared sorrow. I am by nature an introvert but felt comforted

by publicly sharing our mutual love for our daughter.

Dr. Ken Doka put forth great ideas on how newly bereaved should use their support people well. He asks us to think of our support network as doers, listeners, honest evaluators, and respite persons to help in our grief journey. The doers are those you can count on to do whatever you need done without question. Then there are the listeners who are the people you can call or meet, and they will just listen to you without judgment or advice. They witness your story with their quiet presence.

Next are honest evaluators for when you do want advice. These are, first and foremost, people who "get grief." Lastly, the respite people are those who are there for you when you need a break from grieving who can just give you space and help you get some relief from thinking about or talking about the loss. Support persons are critical during these times to provide relief for us both physically and mentally. Recognize early who these people are. Create your own posse if you need to.

I would add that it is also helpful to identify prayer partners if prayer brings comfort to you. It's a peaceful practice for the one praying to feel as though they are doing something kind for those suffering.

Order the chaos through ritual

Dr. William Hoy (2013), author of *Do Funerals Matter?* draws on a vast body of research, showing the importance of ritual in one's initial bereavement. He reminds us of the power in shared stories and the support through gathered community. Countless other authors and researchers highlight the way in which ritual brings order to the chaos from the news of death.

Due to the pandemic, some of our traditional support methods and rituals surrounding death had to be improvised to some extent. Many mourners had to postpone services altogether depending on the spiking of cases and the area of the country lived in. If we were fortunate to have some assemblance, such as a funeral, many churches and funeral homes had changed policies and procedures in 2020 to stay in line with the state's public health orders. Churches could not offer luncheons at times, for example, when the active variant of COVID-19 was high.

After a funeral Mass in many faiths, typically the women's auxiliary will host a luncheon for all who attend. When Kevin's brother, Mark, died in November 2020, we were able to have a funeral Mass but no traditional luncheon. Kevin notes:

> I wanted so badly to talk with all those who made time to come out and some who drove a great distance to be there for us. Those who came and attended also most likely wanted to speak in person to us to share their stories. But after the Mass, we all just walked to our cars, masked and socially distanced, and headed home with our grief. It almost felt like a disservice to my brother, as this is where you share stories about him and what he meant to people. It would have been so valuable for us to laugh and remember together with those who knew him as we process all our grief from the suddenness of the loss.
>
> There was no immediate burial because he wanted cremation, so no gathering around the gravesite initially either. I felt so lost, as this just wasn't normal, as we headed back home. We search for normalcy, we need ritual and tradition, and it was like a life story with no ending, no last chapter. At a later date, we did gather at the graveside to inter the cremains, however, with a much smaller group of people and a few memorable stories.

The agony of loose ends tends to leave one bewildered by the experience of loss. Rituals we once took for granted were also taken from us. It is only then that we realize their value as Kevin shares his sense of being "lost." This was not the normal trajectory after we gathered people together. The perceived support of others provides a type of security and reassurance to the mourner that they are not alone, now or in the future days, weeks, months, and years ahead.

Anna Louise's services in February 2020 were not impacted as the pandemic had not yet been declared. However, with our cousin Wade's in July 2020, everything was altered. I decided to give the immediate family their privacy in the home hospice experience, but all the while, I was praying, packing, and planning to arrive shortly after the news was delivered. I showed up after learning of his death, to find my cousin, his spouse, dazed and pacing in her kitchen. The death was expected, and partial plans were in place. It is hard to consider all the arrangements that will have to be made immediately after the death. She did not remember the next steps. Together, even during a pandemic where we needed to think of so many other precautions, we began to pick up the pieces. Our lives were once again in disarray.

Support of close family and friends was greatly valued, especially in the days, weeks, and months immediately after the death. However, things don't always go as we would hope. Here, Debra explains:

> The surprise, and you might say shock, came my way in a lack of support from a few close people. The undermining of a plan to have a funeral because of the pandemic when the professional funeral director and all those close others in Wade's life for over three decades (professional peers for 32 years) agreed to go forward was puzzling. These few people, with their opposition, added another layer of distress for me and made the grief unbearable. They wanted to wait and have something later when perhaps it was safer to do so. I postponed the funeral for two weeks initially, but the professionals assured me it was safe to gather. There was one family member who was an exception and encouraged me to go forward

noting that it was unlikely that there would be a good turnout at a much later date.

We were at the point in the pandemic where we could socially distance, wear masks, and many places had proper air filtration systems in place (the funeral home) to allow for us to follow guidelines, so we went ahead. It was still hard to process those who questioned my judgement on whether to proceed with a funeral service. As I reflect now, it may be that some people did not want me to be recognized as the chief mourner, yet I was his wife of 23 years and his primary caregiver in this illness.

Most close support persons are helpful, but when families suffer wounds either from childhood scars (i.e., divorce, blended families, alcoholism) or other rifts and traumas, the disruption and chaos are intensified. These people add salt to the wound and interrupt the natural progression of grief. They can be heartless in acknowledging the immediate needs of the chief mourners, those who are closest to the deceased and most affected by the loss.

Disruption from natural death after a life long-lived takes on a different form. My mother's death from old age was an interruption to making memories with her, one we knew was inevitable given her age. When she took her last breath in late October 2020, the daze and interruption we experienced was coupled with adrenaline.

We (my sister, maternal cousin, and I) had just witnessed the active dying and last breath of someone we had cherished for decades. This decline for Mom was seen over a period of months. She knew instinctively that her days were ending on this earth, and she was ready. She made sure everyone knew this, including her doctor. We set up palliative care in her home and hospice followed.

At the very end, there were several days with little to no sleep for any of us. Mom often called out our names and wanted to hold our hands, so we took turns around the clock for days to ensure she felt surrounded by family and not alone in her dying. We dragged mattresses to the living room just outside her room to try to rest our bodies as we attempted to tune out the labored breathing pattern, which we knew signaled "soon." And then there were the amazing hospice professionals stopping by at all hours to reassure us of medication dosages and reminding us that all signs showed "close to death." We cherished every moment with her, praying, crying, and singing to her.

In life, Mom was not a crier. She had often reminded me, "When you cry, you cry alone" as she loved to make you laugh, and she loved to see a reaction (disapproval, as she knew I am a crier). When all three of us were crying in her last moments, I reminded her, "Mom, we are not crying alone. We are here crying together. We love you!" As her hand slipped out of mine, we knew she was gone, and she knew she was surrounded by love and prayer in her own home. We finished strong and will always have a sense of peace about her end-of-life care and about her death.

Because it was an early morning/night death, it took hours for the undertakers to come and escort her from her home to their home. The pure exhaustion afterward and sudden lack of providing round-the-clock care somehow collided with adrenaline and made it nearly impossible to shut down for any sleep.

We sat at her kitchen table together, at 4:00 a.m. and for the first time in our lives in her home, had our hot tea without her beautiful presence. I remember how often, when we received any news, whether it was good or bad, Mom always went to the stove, boiled the water, let the tea kettle scream, and proceeded to pour the hot tea generously. We held this tradition to allow time for us to accept the enormity of what had just happened.

Life was interrupted. Feelings of relief, exhaustion, and sadness collided and consumed us. This caregiving experience for our mom was not viewed as an unwelcome disruption, rather, an incredible honor. Others in the family had their lives on hold as they waited to process the feelings as Brother Jeff recalls:

> The tasks of everyday life were halted as we
> knew Mom was actively dying. The news was

numbing…I thought about how I did not want to see my parents go, but then when I recalled all their struggles due to old age, I didn't want that for them either. The hardest part is never being able to talk with Mom again or that opportunity to listen to her wisdom, wit, charm, and motherly guidance that provided so much love and support.

Death itself once again disrupted our lives, and COVID-19 protocols made it even more challenging for people to gather and feel safe, as we had yet to have a vaccine. Many people reached out with condolences and apologized for not being able to attend the services. Had it not been for these circumstances, the church would have been packed as Mom had a wide reach and a love for all. The pandemic interfered with people's sense of security and safety. We felt cheated as we wanted to see a packed church, which would have contributed to a much more glorious and fitting funeral for this beautiful soul.

With brother Mark's sudden death from COVID-19 in November 2020, we had more of a helpless feeling of disruption. He was in an Intensive Care Unit, being cared for by devoted medical professionals while we waited, hoped, and prayed. The phone call was surreal, and the world as we knew it, the changed world, came to a complete halt. We felt frozen, isolated, and powerless.

We were restricted from going to the family because of the contagion (and vulnerability due to age and exposure and no vaccines), so we waited in our daze for the next phone calls to come through. We notified and disrupted our children's lives with the news, hearing agony in their voices. Their cries by phone showed their great love for their uncle and his family. Not being able to come together and physically touch and hug left us empty.

A sense of overwhelming sadness and raw pain entered our lives again. Yet we used this interruption to deepen our faith in a God of love and peace through prayer. Supporting Mark's wife and family took top priority, but the traditional way in which we could have provided support was disrupted because of the pandemic.

It was late November when Mark died, and I can remember Thanksgiving dinner 2020 as the quietest, most solemn and sad holiday ever for my husband and his family and for us. During most of the dinner, we felt paralyzed. Yet we gave thanks for everything we could think of, the people we still had, the memories of all those we had lost, the life we have left to live, and the hope to weave the legacies of Anna, Wade, Mom, and Mark into the rest of our days.

The ache we experienced from losing all four of these family members within a nine-month period in the middle of disorderly times was, and is, a great deal to bear in our bereavement. Our grief was altered because of a contagion and the necessary restrictions it brought.

Blindsided in the aftermath

Another form of disruption can come in the way of dysfunction in families. Personal experiences coupled with stories from bereaved others attest to how much more painful the impending loss or the loss in the aftermath is when family members do not respect each other's grief in the circumstances.

As some of us processed the news of the loss of multiple family members, there was an unexpected lack of understanding and compassion from people we thought were going to be of great support in tough times. After all, they always had been. This, too, blindsided us and added more disruption. Had I known what the year would bring, perhaps it would not have felt so chaotic and hard to manage, but that is just not the way life works. There was no preparation for what was to come in the way of personal disagreements in everything, from planning the service to attending to details such as the writing of an obituary.

Often, there is little to no forewarning when bad news will come our way or when relationships and perceived support will falter. Given this unpredictability, having a strong support system in place is ideal but oftentimes, as noted, can likewise prove to be greatly disappointing when those you counted on are not there for you. As a result, I have learned to surround myself more with people who exhibit genuine love and care toward others and whose focus is on alleviating pain and distress in other people's lives. They have a deep respect for healthy relationships, are empathic, and know your values.

I cannot stress enough here how critical it is to know that your support persons understand the value of empathy. It starts with listening but goes much deeper. Next, one must often challenge preconceived notions and biases and consider another person's point of view. It involves a level of emotional intelligence. It is the ability to stand in someone else's shoes and see the experience through their eyes. For various reasons, some people never truly become empathetic. They may not like the reality of what the other person is describing, so they are dismissive and blame the other for distorting events.

I find myself evaluating my support persons on a regular basis. I have talks with them often and go over my values and beliefs with them, as these are vital elements in providing solid support to others in distressing times. Above all else, it is critical that one's support persons have an excellent understanding of the process of loss and are nonjudgmental.

Some people will never accept that the disruption right before their eyes is related to the loss or potential loss. Having a good understanding of the myriad of ways in which people express or withhold grief reactions and how we vary in how and when we work through loss experiences is the first step toward preventing the disruption in the first place.

Healthy communication and trust come into play here. No one person should assume that "taking charge" is the right path when it comes to family decision-making, unless there is evidence of wrongdoing, which should involve a family meeting. Another exception for taking charge can be applied if there are no other family members who were legally assigned to attend to matters or if they are unwilling. We do know that when people are in high emotion, they often make bad decisions, may have mistrust for others without evidence, and proceed to take charge without regard for others, which has the potential to destroy lifelong relationships.

Knowing one's place in a family is also critical to preserving relationships and, if not respected, can wreak havoc and cause more disruption. In the case of relationships, great loss may occur after a death when people betray you, act out in high emotion, or simply, they do not "have your back" when wrongdoing occurs and you rightfully expected their support. Often, we are caught off guard and may not even realize these betrayals until we contemplate in the weeks, months, and even years ahead the magnitude of the deeds and misdeeds.

During the chaos, we may feel stunned and get caught up in getting through the challenges presented. I recall a wise quote from one of my favorite celebrities, Oprah Winfrey, who reminds us that "challenges are gifts that force us to search for a new center of gravity. Don't fight them. Just find a new way to stand." This is good advice to look at these challenging circumstances as teaching moments that ultimately make us stronger in the face of adversity.

Grief often creates a feeling of disorder as many emotions clash. Some individuals try to gain control in order to bring things back into order. This behavior, if a person is unaware, has the potential to cause even more disruption. Some seek to gain control of whatever they can, which may include the belongings, the finances, and even the control of other people in order to lessen the feeling of chaos for themselves. Oftentimes, this only adds to the commotion created by the death.

I knew in order to find a balance, I must first contemplate the varied grief styles within the family and learn to respect our differences. I have always been observational, long before I was equipped with sociological theory and research tools. Stepping back from my circumstances, examining not only my own experience but that of the whole (the family) was a norm for me.

In discussion with family members, whose stories lie within these pages, however, some are telling me that they are not in this same space (contemplation). This is understandable, as we are all grieving different relationships. Some of us, depending on the closeness to the deceased, stay in spaces for longer than others. This is where we respect differences and know that not all will describe the working through of grief as I do, or experience it in similar fashion. Having a "sense of emptiness" is not always a part of people's grief journey. Surrendering is not always an option, as some feel as though they might be abandoning the deceased. This place of contemplation may not be recognized for years until one looks back on the experience. Widowed cousin Debra notes:

> It has now been eighteen months since my husband died, and I feel as though I am still in the process of contemplation because I am starting to put pieces together by going through some of his personal and professional paperwork and files (4 file cabinets full). This activity I do alone, and it does help me to make some sense out of the timeline for his dementia illness. There are clues which are helping me to fit the puzzle together. When someone is diagnosed with this type of dementia, you go back in time, thinking of episodes and events that might have signaled the beginning, which is important in constructing the story.
>
> So until I have more of the pieces of the story constructed, it is hard to see myself really in a contemplative place with the whole of this experience of illness, death, and my bereavement. I advise people to be patient with themselves as this all takes time.

Being patient with ourselves and others in the grief journey is paramount to alleviating stress for all involved and for finding peace. One important recognition is that we all have different relationships to grieve and varying strategies for coping, which all have the potential to lead to a healthy outcome.

Respecting differences: styles of grief

Respect for each other, the bereaved, and for the dead means communicating in a way that lessens the disruption and reduces additional suffering. It honors the grief of others in the family, in particular the chief mourners and immediate heirs who most often had the longest and strongest bonds with the deceased.

It is also important that we recognize how scholars have identified "styles of grief." Dr. Ken Doka and Terry Martin's work highlights the difference between "intuitive" and "instrumental" ways in which people process loss. Keep in mind that these styles or types are not a measure of how much the person we lost was loved. Those who exhibit a more intuitive grieving style often express their grief through affect. They develop more emotional symptoms and handle the loss mainly by sharing their feelings with others. They are more likely to attend grief therapy sessions and/or support groups, whereas instrumental grievers are not likely to express emotion. Rather, they attempt to master their feelings and their environment. They use a more cognitive, problem-solving approach and are much more likely to direct their energy into activities (such as work).

The bereaved parents quoted in this book on the loss of their daughter are both suffering. Maureen's husband, Jeff, exhibits more of an instrumental way of processing the loss, through keeping grief private and staying busy, while she is more of an intuitive griever, expressing emotion and wanting to talk things through, such as the events of her daughter's life or the impact she made on others' lives— although the way in which the grief is being processed is shifting and changing for both of them as they move through time and carry their grief.

This concept of styles of grief is best understood as one that lies on a continuum and helps us to understand that an intuitive grief style involves external expressions of emotions as a reflection of the internal emotion. This may be done by openly crying in public settings (such as at a grief support group) so that one's grief is witnessed. Intuitive grievers may cherish the sacred connection to the deceased's belongings more than others, as they may think of the memory connected to the item. This does not mean they value things over people; rather, quite the opposite, they value the memory of the person who cherished the belonging. Often, they want to preserve their legacy and the relationship in some way.

Those who grieve instrumentally often have a more inward experience of their grief with more thinking rather than feeling. They may express grief through doing, in a more physical way than an emotional one. These styles of grief can overlap as well, when at times one is intuitive and at other times, they may exhibit a more instrumental way of grieving. Again, as people move through the grief, this behavior may shift and change.

Unique and altered grief

Moving through grief under ordinary circumstances requires attention not only to our emotional well-being but to our physical, spiritual, and social health as well. In these past few years when our world was chaotic, working through our losses was more of a challenge than the grief process of other significant losses. Many of us did not have traditional support. Some of us had to adjust rituals, while others postponed funeral services altogether. Our needs as chief mourners were not met as we had expected, and as a result, more people are experiencing a prolonged and exceptional grief journey. Some of us do not find ourselves in a "new normal"; rather, we see an abnormal reality. The lack of physical touch, such as hugs, for example, during 2020 in our initial bereavement led to more isolation and a less secure sense of support.

The uncertainty of our everyday routines and the commotion from COVID-19 continues to bring confusion and unwelcome change. When your heart is heavy with grief and sadness, you crave the familiar. But when the familiar can no longer be experienced, such as celebrating holidays and major life events traditionally, things get even more complicated. There is some sense of a parallel universe as the life in which we had lived was/has changed because of the death in the family and then again because of a global pandemic. Initial grief sometimes feels like you are living in an alternate reality, one in which you cannot escape. But when the world has changed, it is even more disorienting. The first bad news in 2020 of Anna's untimely death just before the world was shut down was unwelcome and indescribable. We entered into a changed world without a choice with heavy hearts.

Bearing loss with the backdrop of a pandemic and an uncertain world has, in my view, prolonged, delayed, and complicated grief for many. We had to go into survival mode for our own mortality, which felt as if we were betraying those we lost, as we were distracted from our own grief at times. Typically, we hear bereaved persons ask, "How can the world keep going when I just lost (my son, my spouse)?" But when the world has changed on such a large scale, as we experienced, there is much more of a challenge. Because of the pandemic landscape, we hear, "I lost my best friend and husband, and the whole world changed. Why go on?"

We naturally tell people who are dealing with loss to consider creating a new routine as their identity may need to be reconstructed (i.e., losing a spouse and sharing the same living space or providing caregiving, which is now gone). However, when we must adapt to limited gatherings, wear face coverings, socially distance and isolate more, it is hard to know where to start with a "new routine."

In the early days and months of the pandemic, death from a virus about which much was unknown shocked us all, and we had yet to develop a vaccine. So much uncertainty, misinformation, and division among the general public that had spilled over into the immediate family all proved to be disheartening. One challenge that often accompanies loss is the misunderstanding of what the experience of bereavement involves. This can result from a lack of experience with grief, from our cultural messages, or in some instances, an unwillingness on the part of the support person to see it for what it is.

The lack of understanding by people we love is often more hurtful than one can bear and unfortunately falls on the bereaved person, adding more stress. So how do we help each other while grieving with this backdrop? Here, our bereaved mom Maureen shares her heartache and struggle in this new landscape with how to accept support, what helped, and what did not:

> Mere weeks after my daughter's memorial service, the pandemic hit. It seemed like the entire nation shut down. Travel was severely restricted, businesses implemented limits on gatherings, schools went to online learning, lives were thrown into chaos. I live far away from all of my family and most of my closest friends. Visiting in person was not an option. I had also lost my job working from home because of the pandemic. My hypervigilant focus on my daughter's care was gone. All of those things contributed to an emotional collapse. The saying about that which does not kill you makes you stronger is a cliché that needs to go away.
>
> I essentially spent six months in bed. I had no desire to go out other than essential trips. I did not have the energy to speak to anyone. But I still needed for them to reach out to me. I certainly did not make it easy, as people are not mind readers and most likely presumed that I wanted to be left alone.

As noted earlier, however, she did appreciate the gestures of texts and emails from people who checked in on her. She wanted her privacy, and the pandemic restrictions allowed for this. At the same time, she needed for the loss to be acknowledged and for the stories of Anna to be told. There was a desire to capture the essence of who her daughter was and to ensure she would never be forgotten. She also noted to me several times that she was grateful for the face masks as they hid her sorrowful face. The masks helped conceal her look of despair.

Debra, a retired social worker, who lost her husband Wade in July of 2020 (before vaccinations) brings light to how challenging it was for her to resume life with the backdrop of a pandemic after the funeral.

It was extremely hard to create a new routine in a pandemic. I would get up in the morning and stumble around the house because I could not go to the gym. I could not have my life back because of the virus. I kept thinking…I need to create a routine, but a routine for what? To feed myself? For sitting around the house? For watching the news? I did get out and walk, and when the snow came, I went out and skied. I think today, well over a year after he died, I still struggle with the idea of "routine," especially now in the winter months.

I cannot go to a college class I wanted to attend. It's hard to have the social contacts. I go to the gym because I just have to do something, but then the fear of contracting the virus at my age even with a vaccine is unsettling. I do have a dog who brings comfort, but my social contacts are limited, most connections are made by phone, and my kids pop in and out now; but I think it makes my grief harder; it lingers on because I cannot create the routine that I had hoped to, which means little to no social connection.

The only real, meaningful connection a few months after Wade died was to be able to share in end-of-life caregiving for my maternal Aunt, who was dying. I was able to help my cousins with caregiving because I had been freed of mine for Wade.

It's all just so disappointing. I daydreamed a lot during my husband's illness, of all the things I like to do and would look forward to doing at the end of all this caregiving. It was a sort of preparation for me and a reminder that when Wade died, I would be fine. But I'm not, because I cannot travel as I had hoped or go places I had envisioned.

Some days I feel as though my personal life is falling apart and the whole world is crumbling. In some sense, I feel like Wade's illness was a partial lockdown for a number of years. As his illness progressed, it became harder to "live life" as we knew it. It was easier to stay home.

I heard that you must learn a "new normal" after your spouse dies. But there is nothing normal about our world right now with the pandemic, global warming, political division and more. And I hear news media saying that we have to figure out how to adjust to our "new normal" because of Covid-19, but again, I can't seem to locate any sense of normalcy between the grief and the world conditions.

Many others are still feeling the effects of our changed world and their changed lives due to loss. We have lost our footing. As Debra noted, during those long caregiving years, the daydreaming about what she would do after he was gone helped her to know that there would still be life left for her to live. But now, a year after his death, she asks:

What kind of life is this? I can't do the things I dreamed of because of the continued contagion, even though I am vaccinated and boosted. Reinfection is possible, and I've already had Covid-19 and do not wish to be sick or have the long-term health problems associated with it as I am aging. To say that I am frustrated is an understatement. I am angry and now depressed.

Now, more than ever, we need better infrastructure in our mental health care system, which seems to be failing us for many reasons, some beyond our control. The sheer number of bereaved individuals whose lives were disrupted by a death during the pandemic are cause enough to be concerned. This continued long suffering has led to a barrage of needs for people who are living with the disruption. At the very least, we need to try to understand it and equip people with strategies to persevere through it.

Key takeaways

Locate or create support persons: doers, listeners, honest evaluators, and respite persons (prayer partners).

Hold rituals.

Provide support in some way to each other and to the chief mourners.

Be aware of your place in the bereaved family.

Respect one another's unique way of moving through loss.

Create a new routine to bring order to the chaos.

Recognize and accept the unique and altered grief.

PART II

Perseverance

CHAPTER 4

Suffering

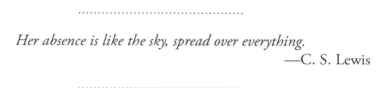

Her absence is like the sky, spread over everything.
—C. S. Lewis

As vulnerable human beings, our experiences of living life and beholding death include suffering. Whether we suffer from physical illness during life or at its end in our dying, it is inevitable. Mental anguish is also part of our human condition. Some of us push through various types of suffering with great courage and perseverance, while others turn to "ugly coping" such as masking pain with unhealthy substances or behaviors.

Regardless of the origin of suffering, no one can escape it during life as humans. During times of significant loss, sorrow and change arrive simultaneously. Here, most humans desire to make sense out of the suffering they are enduring in order to adapt to the changes and hopefully lift the sadness.

In addition, oftentimes, unexpected suffering comes as we watch those whom we love decline. Harold Ivan Smith, a prolific writer in the field of grief studies, attests to this witnessing of our own helplessness that brings great sadness and suffering our way. In his book on the loss of his own father, he reflects.

> It was so hard for me to see him suffering. To see him stripped of his strength. To see the pleading in his eyes. This once strong man, now a feeble, frail shell of what he had been: robust, healthy, strong. (Smith, p. 108).

These events occurring in the caregiving or visits with those we love who are dying often become part of our story of loss as we process the suffering both they and we endure.

Search for meaning

For many bereaved individuals, it is through a search for meaning in their current circumstances that they learn to process loss. For some, this search involves a painful look back and a stark realization that no more memories will be made with the deceased. Psychologist and grief scholar Dr. Robert Neimeyer stresses the importance of meaning making and notes that this search for meaning "is a central construct that links other contemporary theories of grief together."

One of these contemporary theories is known as *Attachment Theory* and was developed by John Bowlby (1958). It is concerned with affectional bonds between people and their origins in childhood and adolescent relationships and the separation of these bonds or by their defective development. Research studies show that compared to people with secure styles of attachment, those with one of the insecure styles (dismissing, avoidant, preoccupied/anxious, or disorganized) will most likely experience more challenges in the grief process and less post-traumatic growth (Cohen and Katz 2015).

Another contemporary theory is *Assumptive World Theory*, which was initially established by Colin Murray Parkes (1988) and refers to a conceptual system, developed over time, that provides us with expectations about the world and ourselves. Janoff-Bulman (1992) carried it further as she went on to identify three core assumptions that shape our worldview: that the world is benevolent, the world is meaningful, and the self is worthy (p. 6). Therefore, when trauma occurs, violent tragedy and death, for example, each of these assumptions are challenged, and the loss of this assumptive world can occur (Kaufmann 2002b). In 2020 we were thrown a curveball, in that the world was in lockdown and chaos as we all feared for our lives. So our assumptive world was unraveling before the deaths occurred in our families. When the family deaths came, the assumptive world was truly shattered.

Additionally, there is the *Dual Process Model* put forth by Stroebe and Schut (1999), who identify two types of stressors for the grieving individual, loss and restoration oriented, along with a dynamic, regulatory coping process of oscillation. They describe this as where one at times confronts, and at other times avoids, the various tasks of grieving. They suggest that adaptive coping includes the confrontation-avoidance of loss and the restoration stressors. In addition, the model contends the need to take respite from dealing with either of the stressors as an essential part of adaptive coping.

The authors suggest that this fluctuation between processing painful memories and doing the necessary activities of daily living, for example, cannot be done at the same time; therefore the survivors oscillate between emotion-focused (loss oriented) and task-focused (restoration oriented) grief.

All three contemporary theories link together with Dr. Neimeyer's meaning making framework. The latter shows how one constructs meanings about the self and about the world through narratives and relationships. This may include finding or creating a sense of understanding with regard to a loss (sense making), creating meaning structures that highlight positives resulting from a loss (benefit finding), along with positive or negative reconstruction of the self (identity change). The search often includes the painful assessment of memories past, as well as those lost in the present and for those that will not be made in the future. Widow Debra imagines the upcoming milestones of her grandchildren and the absence of her deceased spouse, Wade, at those events as she tries to make sense of the loss, find benefit, and work on her new identity.

> Now, at the two-year mark after my husband's death, I think about the things he would

have been proud of if he were still here. Recently, our high school-age granddaughter won an exceptional award, and in part, it was due to his efforts. He found joy in taking her to attend a program to learn about the possibilities and opportunities. He saw it as his job to ensure her chances for the future. He would have been so very proud of this achievement. He also took her to every father-daughter dance as her biological father is not active in her life.

Wade with his granddaughters, Jayda, and Breanna

She sighs, pauses, and then continues.

Some days I go outside and sit on the porch of our cottage and think, why is he not here to enjoy the life we built together? He felt so good about what we had built. But now, I am building the future alone. And then there's the fact that he was a doer and a planner, and it seems now there are a million things, and he's not here to take care of any of it. I took his role for granted. But, for me, the big thing here is that I ask myself, What am I teaching my two adult daughters and my grandkids as I recreate my identity as a new widow? My widowhood is complicated because in those last few years, there were things that were hurtful, and so I am still constructing the past and piecing it all together. I ponder how much of what was said to me by my now deceased husband was truly coming from him, or was it from his Lewy body dementia.

In some ways, as I try to make sense of it all, the stress lessens, and I try not to dwell on any one particular incident; rather, I am thankful that things didn't progress into something tragic. He had the same diagnosis as Robin Williams, and it can be unbearable to imagine all the possibilities as you are moving through it.

At the core of this suffering, we often find regrets, guilt, and a lack of joy in life. Well-intended people remind us that our grief is the expression of continued love for who we lost. Given that our love cannot be expressed directly to them any longer because they died, this love has no place to go and is not reciprocal, which can result in a deep void. Suffering brought on by loss can be an occasion to connect more deeply with someone or something, such as a higher power, God, the universe, whatever our source of strength and comfort is. But we can also connect on a new level with those who died, through cemetery visits, memorial tattoos, wearing their jewelry, and many other contemporary tributes to carry on a bond and create legacy for them.

Acknowledging regret and guilt

Numerous feelings and emotions after a loss can get diminished by others, which brings a unique pain. Regrets, for example, are common and need to be voiced and heard as well as honored and not lessened. Guilt feelings over lost opportunities with the deceased can result in strong emotions. They, too, should be recognized and acknowledged when mentioned, although most support people want to diminish comments made about regret by the bereaved to feel as though they are helping ease the suffering for them. Quite the contrary. The more these normal feelings and emotions are reduced, the more agonizing it can be for the griever as they don't feel supported.

When feelings expressed need to be accepted and honored, the bereaved can face them and eventually move forward when ready with a recognition of accepting the missed opportunity. If a griever asks you for a strategy to reduce the feelings of guilt, then advice is warranted, but we should still normalize the feelings of guilt for others, not dismiss them when originally aired. In time, there may be an opportunity to explore them more deeply to see if they are justified or not.

Many people also have an uncomfortable feeling when a bereaved person is expressing sadness for too long (in our view). It is common to try to ease the suffering of others in various ways, but oftentimes, it comes across to the griever as a constant evaluation of their grief and even as a judgment for them that they should be moving along faster in the grief journey.

I learned a great deal from the work of Horwitz, a sociologist, and Wakefield, a social worker, who wrote extensively on this observation in their book *The Loss of Sadness: How Psychiatry Transformed Normal Sorrow into Depressive Disorder* (2012). These authors show how human sadness has been viewed as an abnormal experience in our culture and how quick we are to medicalize this human emotion. They illustrate how psychiatry no longer clearly differentiates between normal sadness and depressive disorder.

To this point, I remember getting a prescriptive email (while working for a small academic institution), which went out to all employees. A fellow coworker, at age thirty-four, had died the evening before from a sudden heart attack. We were stunned. But we were even more shocked by the message from the family in the same email. They were asking us all to leave behind the sadness and tears and join them for a "Celebration of Life" in his memory just days after the news. We were all very sad, naturally, and having a hard time controlling our emotions. The message sent out was so conflicting that very few people attended, as they felt they would not be able to hold back their tears and sadness over the death of a young man who had just become a father.

Although it is understandable to want to celebrate a life now gone, it is important to both *mourn the death* and *celebrate the life.* The reality is that we are more than likely both sad and shocked, and it is challenging to manage all emotions at a service. The current culture is creating a climate of celebration by noting "that is what the deceased would want," but it clashes with how we really feel and makes grief harder to move through in my view.

I am reminded of the wise words of Dr. William Hoy in *Do Funerals Matter?* who tells us that "the bereavement process *inevitably* includes sadness. Suggesting that mourners should get into a 'celebratory' mood is a thinly veiled attempt to deny the pain of grief" (p. 131). We must accept the deep sadness that grief can bring our way as natural. Attempts to thwart it will only make it resurface later.

Silent presence from support persons

We often have good intentions with our words when trying to lift sadness and suffering for others who are grieving. Witnessing the person's emotions with our silent presence, however, is much more helpful. Allowing them to come to terms with the sorrow is beneficial. I asked my sister-in-law, Maureen, to write about her suffering as a way to enlighten us not only on the suffering felt from the loss of an adult daughter but also to share her insight on what might have been more supportive for her and her family over these past few years.

Here's what she is experiencing in early 2022, two years into her grief:

> My suffering is intense…I wake up every day asking God why I am still here. I go through my days as if in an episode of *The Twilight Zone.* I function but barely. I was a dedicated runner for 27 years, but what used to be a physical and

mental release for me now triggers flashbacks and stops me in my tracks. I used to find joy in simple things but will now settle for fleeting respite from my grief. When I run errands like grocery shopping, I seek out stores with self-checkouts so I don't have to interact with people. I feel like a fraud when I speak to strangers, like I am an actor playing a part of a happy person.

My grief has been met with wildly varying reactions. I have a very small group of people who have been lifelines for me, who I can trust with sharing my grief, who empathize without judgment. I have been surprised by the number of friends from my past with whom I had lost contact with but still check in with me occasionally just to see how I am doing. I have been saddened by people I thought I was close to who have not contacted me beyond offering initial condolences. I have had people attempt to direct my grief. I have heard every cliché and platitude, many of them more than once. The people who have helped me the most are the ones who ask me simple open-ended questions like, "how are you doing?" or "what can I do to ease your pain, even if for only a moment?" or simply say "tell me more about your daughter" or "I am thinking about you." Those acts allow me to be my authentic, unguarded self and have literally saved my life more than once.

I have found solace in music, especially songs that connect me with my daughter. On Fridays my sister and I share long-distance dance parties, carrying on a ritual that my daughter and I loved. We choose a mutual song earlier in the week and play it for my daughter. I hope she can hear it and laugh at our bad lip-synching and dancing.

I have never enjoyed talking on the phone, and I do not have any social media accounts. What I have found helpful is receiving texts or e-mails. I can respond on my own schedule, consider what I want to share or not share, even control how my mood is perceived.

Many people shared inspirational text messages with me. Those could be anything from cards to books to Bible quotes. The actual messages were not comforting to me, but the thought and effort by the people sending them was. I did not expect anyone to say something that would magically dissolve my grief. Even if attempts at support were clumsy or awkward, I still appreciated the intent behind them.

Acknowledgment of suffering for this bereaved mom was (and still is) important even though the communication mode might be viewed as minimal. It became critical to her well-being and development of perseverance for others to acknowledge her loss and to show concern.

Unnecessary suffering

Sadly, sometimes additional *unnecessary* suffering typically caused by others during these difficult times can wreak havoc in these situations and prolong our grief. It may come in the way of people who just do not understand loss, their own and/or that of others. They may be uncomfortable with expressed emotion and think they must alleviate it with their advice or clichés. Or it occurs when people tend to think the bereaved should grieve the way they do. It's important to know that not everyone cries, not everyone gets angry, not everyone starts a foundation in the memory of the deceased. Some grievers do all of this, and yet others choose another path.

Grief is as unique as our fingerprint. You don't have to cry to be considered as in the depths of grief. We learned earlier about styles of grief, instrumental and intuitive, the work of Dr. Ken Doka and Terri Martin, that help us to better understand and respect differences.

At other times, great suffering is felt through the inappropriate actions of others without regard for the unique ways in which people grieve in the family. I have heard numerous stories from families and have spoken to varied professionals working in the death and grief fields including chaplains and clergy. They discuss how countless families are divided after a death because of the hurtful words, accusations, and inappropriate actions of people they thought they knew well. Loss brings people together in high emotion where some want to bring order to the chaos and sometimes inappropriately seek to gain control of everything they can (i.e., the possessions, the finances, etc.). Others go into defense because they feel misunderstood. Still others stay silent even in the face of wrongdoing. Families often find themselves asking, *Who are these people?*

These miscommunications and divisions often exhaust the grievers and disrupt a healthy grief trajectory resulting in delayed or prolonged grief and, oftentimes, destruction of lifelong relationships. My advice is to remember to step back, look at the broader picture of relationships, recognize the variation in moving through the grief, and show respect for one another. If the relationships still fail, or if others have little to no self-awareness and continue to cause harm or take away your peace, move on from them graciously. Keep a safe and reverent distance to avoid more hurt as you work through yet even more loss, the relationships.

Some writers I admire remind us that becoming more aware of our actions and inactions is an art that needs to be developed, and we can only do this for ourselves. Bach, in *The Power of Perception*, writes his account in an entire chapter on awareness.

> We develop it by reflection; by seeing, through thought, the commonly unseen. We discover it by association with those who have eyes to see, those to whom it is immaterial whether

the object seen is real or merely the hopeful pro-
jection of an ideal. We improve it by daring to
be fascinated with the childhood wonders of the
searching eye, wonders which mystic minds have
always found intriguing:

"To see the world in a grain of sand,
And heaven in a wild flower;
Hold infinity in the palm of your hand
And Eternity in an hour."

We identify ourselves by finding lessons of
life wherever we go, in whatever we do, and wherever we are—lessons of awareness in such simple
things as a rose in a garden or lilies in the field,
or by daring to conclude from the wonder of little children "theirs is the kingdom of heaven."
(p. 40–41)

And this is where it begins, with an awareness first of the simple
but glorious things around us. Once we have this consciousness of
the world we inhabit, we can develop a personal sense of self-awareness of our words and behaviors and how they help or hinder.

Oftentimes, people who have developed this self-awareness are
humble and encouraging. They are not critical, jealous, or judgmen-
tal of others. They are "second mountain people." You will know
them when you are in their presence. They are peaceful, gentle, kind,
and patient. They have a deep joy. These qualities are captured in
scripture by St. Paul in Galatians chapter 5 who describes them as
the fruit of the Holy Spirit. St. Paul names love, joy, peace, patience,
kindness, goodness, trustfulness, gentleness, and self-control. Some
versions of the Bible also list faithfulness. They, of course, take practice but are what we strive toward as followers of Christ, which aid in
our brotherly relationships.

What I have learned and witnessed is that some relationships,
even though they might have been loving and close before a family
death, can become toxic as noted earlier. Unfortunately, this is much
more common than people realize. When emotions are high and

people are vulnerable, an ability to recognize our own self-centered behavior can be nonexistent. Much of the dysfunction is due to a lack of respect for one another and a complete lack of understanding about how we grieve differently.

Know that there will always be those who either have different values or are so damaged emotionally that they become abusive in these circumstances. You are not obligated to carry on a relationship, even if you are blood-related. I add this here because of the enormous number of stories I have heard over the last decade from the bereaved, many who spend years unsuccessfully making attempts at repair.

This point was also well articulated in a sermon I heard where the priest emphasized how important it is to forgive others and seek reconciliation but also how equally important it is to protect our dignity.

> There are going to be some relationships…
> where mercy can only get us so far, so I do want
> to be clear about reconciliation. When we forgive
> someone, it may mean we have to keep distance.
> If they are a person who consistently hurts us and
> who refuses to change or acknowledge their lack
> of perfection, then absolutely you need to guard
> the treasure that is your human dignity and keep
> a respectful, polite distance, because mercy and
> reconciliation are not the same thing. Jesus tells
> us we have to forgive everyone, but he also explic-
> itly tells us what people we don't reconcile with.
> What's the difference? Reconciliation means the
> relationship is restored.
>
> For reconciliation to work, the aggrieving
> person needs to say, "I ask your forgiveness," and
> they need to show an effort to change. And if they
> don't do that, then polite, respectable distance is
> needed, because what's inside of you, He [point-
> ing to the crucifix] died for you, so you treat it
> with dignity. And if someone else can't, it is not
> an act of love to volunteer for abuse. For us, that

distinction is important…you are the only one who can control mercy and forgiveness inside of you; reconciliation takes two. (Fr. J. Krupp 2021)

Trust must be built back, and this, too, takes time. Until that time comes, respectful distance and prayer are the best tools.

After the initial period of deep suffering from multiple losses and fractured living relationships, I found myself retreating and wanting silence. I called to mind Ecclesiastes 3:1–8:

> For everything there is a season, and a time
> for every matter under heaven:
>> a time to be born and a time to die,
>> a time to plant and a time to uproot,
>> a time to kill and a time to heal,
>> a time to tear down and a time to build,
>> a time to weep and a time to laugh,
>> a time to mourn and a time to dance,
>> a time to scatter stones and a time to gather them,
>> a time to embrace and a time to refrain,
>> a time to search and a time to give up,
>> a time to keep and a time to throw away,
>> a time to tear and a time to mend,
>> a time to be silent and a time to speak,
>> a time to love and a time to hate,
>> a time for war and a time for peace.

Much of the Holy Scripture comes back to how God knows best and wants us to always trust him with all things. I am reminded of the words of another priest, Fr. Richard Rohr in his book, *Falling Upward*, who theorizes:

> Silence is the only language spacious enough
> to include everything and to keep us from slip-
> ping back into dualistic judgments and divisive
> words.

Moving away from the continuous thoughts of the hurtful events that caused additional suffering was a step in the right direction at the right time. Although I knew I'd be back reminiscing on good memories made, the pull was strong to surrender. But I was not exactly sure what I was surrendering, so I did some research and reading while I retreated.

Venerable Marthe Robin, a French Roman Catholic mystic wrote: "Suffering is an unsurpassed school of true love. It is the living language of love and the great teacher of humankind. One learns to love and one does not really love except in and by suffering, for true suffering instructs us, not through human delights, but through the stripping away and renouncing of self on the cross."

David Brooks also writes about the *valley of suffering* in *The Second Mountain.* He suggests that the experiences people have in life that bring them into this space have the potential to break them open.

> These seasons of suffering have a way of exposing the deepest parts of ourselves and reminding us that we're not the people we thought we were. People in the valley have been broken open. They have been reminded that they are not just the parts of themselves that they put on display. There is another layer to them they have been neglecting, a substrate where the dark wounds, and most powerful yearnings live. Some shrivel in the face of this kind of suffering. They seem to get more afraid and more resentful. They shrink away from their inner depths in fear. Their lives become smaller and lonelier.... But for others, this valley is the making of them.
>
> The season of suffering interrupts the superficial flow of everyday life. They see deeper into themselves and realize...there is a fundamental ability to care, a yearning to transcend the self and care for others. And when they have encoun-

tered this yearning, they are ready to become a whole person.

This insight echoes, having been down in the valley myself, where my true self was exposed. The "yearning to transcend" arrives as we look toward helping others or to a cause bigger than ourselves, as Mr. Brooks refers to, where we surrender to the ego. More on that soon, but first, we empty ourselves and let go. This often involves accepting the suffering in our midst.

Redemptive suffering

We have little to no control over the suffering that comes our way. What we do have control over is how we let this pain impact our lives. Great suffering can either transform us or embitter us. For some individuals, suffering makes them the worst version of themselves as they carry forward hatred, bitterness, and resentment and project anger toward others. It also can equip us, however, with the ability to be more compassionate and kinder to others in similar circumstances.

The faith I practice teaches us that suffering is redemptive. My faith community believes that we are all called to unite our suffering with that of Christ. Pope John Paul II reminded us that "Each man, in his sufferings, can also become a sharer in the redemptive suffering of Christ." This facet of my faith I have known all my life, and at times, it is easy to embrace, but at other times, such as with these multiple losses, it is perplexing and challenging.

In early spring 2021, shortly after our family's fourth loss in late 2020, a close friend asked me if I had sought out anyone in my faith community to help me in the search for meaning. Because most of my closest support persons also practice the same faith, I had not pursued anyone outside of my immediate support circle. But this comment gave me pause, and I decided to try to reach out further in the hopes that it could bring me more peace, as I believe that the greater part of grief work involves a spiritual struggle.

Soon after my friend's suggestion, I sought out spiritual guidance by meeting with a young priest at my mother's parish. I gave him the overview of the challenges I was having with working through the grief and my frustration with myself for not being able to understand and see the hand of God in it. I explained that my struggle was not only from the multiple loss but more so over the family dysfunction that began the very day my father died and continues.

I told him I had a good support system in place but that I was getting impatient with myself and others in the family. He asked a few questions and then began to move toward the edge of his seat, announcing, "I know what it is, I know what it is." He was excited, so I stopped talking and thought *Finally, I am going to get some helpful insight here!* I waited as he explained that my suffering was to be embraced and was redemptive in nature. He announced, "You are becoming a saint!" I remember going blank and then trying hard not to laugh as my first thought was *St. Laurel! Well, I have a long way to go.* After a few moments, I said to Father, "Really? Hmm, martyrdom, that is not exactly what I thought you were going to say!" He assured me that his advice was solid.

Why didn't I expect this? After all, this is what the faith has taught me. Frequently, my mother would say "offer it up" when someone was experiencing any kind of pain, from physical or mental anguish. I knew what she meant without explanation from my many years of parochial school education. We were to offer the pain up for the forgiveness of sins. We were taught to ask God for the grace to push through whatever we were experiencing, and at the same time, offer up the pain for various entities, such as the poor souls in purgatory, for the less fortunate, or in reparation for our own sins, and the like. It was also emphasized that this practice must always be done in union with a focus on the passion of Christ as he endured great mental and physical agony and even death for us. It often includes an action of holding onto one's crucifix and other blessed items, such as a scapular[3] (which were more popular in my youth), along with a prayer for strength to endure the pain.

This practice made me more other-centered each time I offered up my own pain without complaint. It helps us surrender our ego and pride so that God's grace can be sufficient. Once I imagined myself on a journey of "sainthood," a transformation began to take shape in terms of surrendering the ego and entering a contemplative state. I was no longer concerned with the repair of relationships as I knew I had to place them and all the woundedness at the feet of God. I stopped trying to be understood by others. God knew my heart and saw it all. I had little desire going forward to have those old relationships back. I was reminded of how some storms come to clear a path for whatever God has next in our lives. There was grace bestowed in that sacrament with the priest. Would I make it to St. Laurel? Time will tell.

Key takeaways for the bereaved

> Searching for meaning in the loss is healthy and typical.
> Regrets and guilt are common and normal.
> Connect with a higher power for comfort and strength.
> Expect people to evaluate your grief process.
> Mourn the death *and* celebrate the life once lived.
> Connect with others experiencing a similar loss.
> Surrender the ego.
> Let suffering transform you.

Key takeaways for support persons

> Your silent presence is important; advice and clichés are not.
> Defer to the "chief mourners" for decisions.
> Become aware of your own responses to loss.
> Respect differences.

---

3   Made of cloth, worn by both religious and laity, that is placed over the shoulders, worn underneath clothing, and has a variety of symbolism, including the constant protection of the Blessed Virgin in life's journey and also at the moment of passing into the fullness of eternal glory.

CHAPTER 5

Emptiness/Surrender/
Contemplation

After months of examining my own grief while supporting my
family in theirs, there was a large pull to lean more into the pain
(instead of questioning it or continuing to make sense of it). At one
point, I thought I could write myself out of it, given that writing is
my go-to and proven to be cathartic, but there was a quick realization
that it was not going to happen. Too much cognitive fog was experienced initially while in deep grief. And with each consecutive loss, it
seemed as though the haze would never lift.

This fog prevented me from the ease of writing with my usual
flow of ideas. Of course, there was resistance through procrastination
("After a long walk I will be more inspired to write."), avoidance
("What's the point of all this anyway?") and a limited belief that my
work was valuable ("Scores of books are being published on grief and
loss."). One day, through an email (Monday Motivator) from the

National Center for Faculty Development & Diversity, I was reminded to name the resistance in order to diffuse the power it had over me. The same held true in relation to my grief.

Naming the strong emotions and feelings as I was experiencing them was very helpful. This is a practice to help manage intense emotion. Dr. Daniel Siegel, a professor, psychiatrist, and codirector of the *Mindful Awareness Research Center at UCLA* identified a technique known as Name It to Tame It. This is where we identify an intense emotion, or name it, which has the potential to reduce the stress and anxiety, or tame it, in the brain and the body where the emotion is causing the reaction. The practice not only brings immediate relief but also supports our ability over time to be with large emotions when they show up without getting swept up in them.

Also, I knew I needed pauses from making sense out of it all. This is an important step to recognize and one that Margaret Stroebe and Hank Schut identified in the Dual Process Model of Grief as noted in the previous chapter, which incorporates an oscillation for respite.

One can only give so much energy to what comes with the grieving of memories and dealing with disruption and suffering before being depleted. I had to work and teach during this time, and although I practiced self-care throughout, I still felt somewhat worn out from the evaluation of my own grief and that of family members whom I love deeply.

I recognized that there was not a healthy work/grief/life balance going on for me. I wondered if having the extensive knowledge from over two decades of study and research related to the experience of bereavement, was, perhaps, not helpful. Sometimes, as professionals may attest, our ability to see the complications of grief because we are equipped with the theoretical knowledge, can cause distress for ourselves.

I could see complicated grief on the horizon for some family members, and I could easily identify the origin of family dysfunction caused solely by the loss. Yet they were both too big to tackle, and those impacted were not receptive to the advice. Surrendering to that inability to help people you love was a hard step.

Our support during this time also has an impact on our movement through the grief. If we have a strong network of listeners who know how to provide us with a healthy dose of non-anxious silent presence, compassion, and empathy, coupled with honest evaluators who can give us feedback when we request it, we may move through the grief much easier. But people surprise us in their inability to be present in a helpful way. This is especially true when the deceased was aged, in the case of my mother, and people think you do not have "as much" grief to process because "you had her for so long, and she lived a full life." Or people are just simply ill-equipped and uneasy around those who are bereaved.

Weak systems of support include those who do not have a good understanding of how to process loss. The hurtful comments will not help, such as "You need to move on. It's been six months." Oftentimes, close family members and friends are uncomfortable watching our sadness and struggle and with good intentions may desire for us to move on. But this lack of respect and consideration of the various ways in which we process loss is counterproductive in terms of support. What results is that the bereaved have to find a way to muster up the strength to comfort themselves. They must operate with a special kind of grace to understand the inability of others, for whatever reason, who are not able to provide help to them in this dark period of their lives.

Organized support groups for those who have few family members or friends or weak systems of support can be very helpful. A caveat here that some group facilitators tend to equip those in attendance with words and phrases, such as "grief triggers" or "the new normal," which don't fit all and often shape the experience of bereavement. Our culture often "prescribes" grief in many ways, such as "She would not want us to be sad" or "Let's focus on *celebrating* her life," which leaves out room for mourning that is a necessary part of our grief. We can do both, and there can be joy right alongside sorrow in our bereavement.

If we truly want to be transformed by the experiences of loss and change, which involve pain and effort to persevere on our part, then, unfortunately, we may have to be the ones who choose the best support to have around us. Notice who takes your peace away and makes grief harder, then distance from them. Keep in mind that we do not always see grief the same way, nor do we move through the loss at the same speed.

Learning to surrender involved not trying to leave the pain but rather to lean more into it, experience it, then live life forward. Allowing for a healthy oscillation between grieving my own emotions (exploring memories) and then attending to tasks (such as my responsibility of being a strong support person in the family) was practiced more.

I looked at and accepted my limitations in supporting those grieving in the family as some indicated they wanted support but on their terms. It's important to respect that, and as a result, peace eventually followed. A sort of "letting go" experience from "holding on" was a necessary step in my journey. I embraced my painful emotions that surfaced because of not being able to provide optimal support in the suffering, both for me and vicariously as I witnessed my family's grief. I accepted that I may never have a complete understanding, that the whys may never be answered, and therefore, it might serve me better to accept that which I could not understand. Each family member knew I was there for them but that ultimately it was their loss to grieve. My support became more hands off, involving more listening and acknowledging and less open evaluating of their grief.

I prayed for grace to be still as I held my favorite biblical verse closely: "Be still and know that I am God" (Psalm 46:10 NRSV). For two reasons, this proved to be somewhat challenging. One, I am an educator, and I tend to intellectualize more than average, so it's hard to quiet the mind. I am always in observation mode in the hope that I can help others who are struggling with loss. Two, I greatly value relationships and enjoy my close support persons' input on my own challenges and struggles to keep me on the right track. But it became clear that the grief now required work in solitude.

Being still in mind, spirit, and body must be practiced. In my field as both a sociologist and a bereavement educator, it is expected that theories learned are to be applied. This entails examining the meanings surrounding individual and group behavior, including verbal and nonverbal communication, in order to effectively understand the situation and what factors are influencing the behavior. But to move through my personal losses, I found that I needed to move more out of my head and into my life more, in particular looking closely at the spiritual component of our human existence. I began by reminiscing about how important the virtue of peace is to me and chose the word *peace* as my sacred word in my centering prayer time practice.

I recalled how as a child, I was guided in parochial schools with instruction from a few laymen teachers along with the Felician Sisters, officially known as the Congregation of Sisters of St. Felix of Cantalice, Third Order Regular of St. Francis of Assisi. I took the time to reexamine the values they had emphasized. They were kind, caring individuals devoted to service and Franciscan values. These teachers all left a love footprint in my heart, and I will always be grateful for the sacrifices my parents made so I could attend a parochial school in my formative years. Eleanor Roosevelt and the opening lines from her poem, "Footprints in Your Heart," rang so true as I thought of my elementary years: "Many people will walk in and out of your life, But only true friends will leave footprints in your heart." These incredible teachers did just that. They befriended their students in a way that we felt very well loved and cared for as we learned.

As young students, we attended Mass daily, and we prayed the prayer of St. Francis of Assisi (c. 1181–Oct. 3, 1226), Italian Catholic friar, deacon, and known mystic. He is one of the most venerated religious figures in Christianity. St. Francis founded the men's Order of Friars Minor, the women's Order of St. Clare, the Third Order of St. Francis, and the Custody of the Holy Land. He is the patron saint for the poor, the sick, and for animals because of the love he showed for all of them. The prayer reads:

> Lord, make me an instrument of your peace;
> Where there is hatred, let me sow love;
> Where there is injury, pardon;
> Where there is doubt, faith

Where there is despair, hope;
Where there is darkness, light
And where there is sadness, joy.

O Divine Master, Grant that I may not so much seek to be consoled as to console; to be understood as to understand; to be loved as to love. For it is in giving that we receive; it is in pardoning that we are pardoned; And it is in dying that we are born to eternal life.

As I grew into my adult years, this prayer became a cherished gift to help me along the life journey, especially in times of distress. Ultimately, this prayer is a plea for peace. I have discovered that the only way to have complete peace is to surrender from the preoccupation of the self, make life brighter and lighter for others, and trust the unknown. But we must arrive there on our own terms and on our own timeline. We must practice self-compassion and listen to our inner stirrings to find true peace.

The second challenge I encountered in attempting to "be still," as noted earlier, was because I greatly value relationships and enjoy objective input with regard to my struggles to keep me on the right track. I love to always have an honest evaluator. That's what friends and close others do to support us through life.

At this time, for personal support, I confided regularly in four people who know and love me well, my husband, my maternal cousin, my sister-in-law out west, and my lifelong friend, Lin. My grief felt safest with them. They were (and still are) empathetic listeners who validate my feelings, which ultimately helped me to live forward. There was never any dismissal of my emotions or suggestions that I have unrealistic expectations; rather, they offered empathy and often advice, if I asked for it.

Hesitantly, I learned how to have some distance and let go of this small but important circle of feedback for a while so that I could delve more deeply into my innermost being to find peace. This involved not having a resolution for some of the problems associated with multiple losses. The peaceful environment of lake life in the summer of 2021 provided the perfect place for solitude and reflection as I read and prayed more and talked with support persons less about my innermost struggles. God and nature became my source and sustained me.

Learning to sit with "not knowing"

I reread the work of Thomas Merton, an American Trappist monk, theologian, mystic, poet, social activist, and scholar of comparative religion, who reminds us in his writing that we do not need to know precisely what is happening or where it is all going. He stressed that we need to recognize the possibilities and challenges offered by the present moment and to embrace them with courage, faith, and hope. His work helped me to see that I had some preconceived notion of how things were supposed to be, which ultimately opened my eyes to embrace the "not knowing."

Eventually, I arrived at a place where I was compelled to imagine myself as an empty vessel. In this space, I had a strong awareness of the importance of being still. Enormous grief had been carried for too long. I once read an interesting definition that "grief is when your arms ache from the emptiness you hold." I have learned that the longer you hold the accumulated grief from multiple loss, the heavier the ache. I followed the strong calling to withdraw daily from the busyness of life and work in order to just be present in my own private space and in nature. I had to learn to sit with the prospect of not knowing. This space provided me with an even greater sense of the need to let go. It is hard to explain to those who have never tried to free themselves of agonizing thoughts of situations out of our control, when the heart is yearning and aching (i.e., if I could have just one more day with Mom; if only they could understand the hurt and permanent damage being done in this relationship, etc.). Surrendering to the unknown took a special grace.

For some, typically men, surrendering means defeat. But from a Christian perspective, surrender means victory. Surrendering is the ability to give yourself solely to something, to flow like water, to not force things. There is no room here for self-doubt. Surrendering brings peace above all understanding. Some of us will be able to let go much easier than others, but again there are variables that contribute to this letting go, in particular the strength of the bond in the relationship, the close contact with them, and our role in their daily lives.

For me, I believe this period of surrender surfaced soon after losing my mother who had provided me with a solid sense of structure and purpose in my adult life, especially in our last five years together. The backdrop here is that prior to Mom's death, my family had lost other very significant family members including my brother Jeremiah in 2014 at the age of sixty-eight. My husband and I had also both lost our fathers at the beginning of 2018, just two weeks apart. These losses were keenly felt and grieved. All three men were strong forces on both sides of the family.

Shortly after my brother's untimely 2014 death, I was offered an academic job in my home state, which I had pursued after witnessing the struggles of my older bereaved parents who were in their eighth decade of life. This new position suited me well so that I could be more present to my own family and provide and organize some shared caregiving for my parents in their old age. It came with sacrifice, however, as I turned down a dream academic position at a Catholic university, knowing in my heart that my parents deserved to have a feeling of security at this stage in their lives. It was all worth it. I would not change a thing.

As the oldest daughter in my family, there was a sense of responsibility and commitment to put their needs first as they had done for me during childhood. The time had come for that last chance at honoring my parents. I wanted to reassure them that I would do everything possible to make the end of their lives as struggle-free as possible. Given that I had worked in end-of-life settings, including palliative care and hospice, and held academic positions where I was required to stay up to date with current research, it was a top priority to provide security for them in this last stage of their lives.

I lived with them in their condominium during this time and stayed through the workweek since the new job was a ten-minute drive from their residence. Siblings, both in and out of state, shared the caregiving, which began chiefly after our father died and Mom needed more help. I was immersed in my parents' daily routine for several years prior to their deaths from old age. As one would imagine, the weeks were filled with dentist and doctor appointments, medical prescription management, meal preparations, meal deliveries, and eventually palliative and hospice care. I remember shortly after my father died, asking my mother, "What will I do when you are gone?" to which she sweetly replied, "Oh, you will be fine and have more time for your family." I took this opportunity to tell her what she meant to me and how she was the best mother on earth. She shifted that compliment back to me, noting that I was a good mom too. I viewed her as my north star, which is why it was such a difficult void when she was gone.

In the immediate months after Mom's death, the emptiness seeped in throughout the initial phases of the grief. But I found myself not giving way to it just yet. On some level, I felt as though my identification as a primary caregiver had left a big gaping hole. Filling up the void with writing or more service to others was attempted but proved to be challenging, and so I put it off and worked on self-care, which saved me. I found walks in nature to be soothing, and my days at the lake were, and still are, a godsend. I was moving into surrender as I had felt beat down from attempts to heal living relationships where family dysfunction was a constant companion and added to the grief.

For some, a sense of emptiness can be profound and sensed sooner, especially when the death is sudden and unexpected. Many bereaved people I have sat with have questioned the meaning of their own mortality after a significant and sudden death of someone loved. There are those who say they are "ready to go" while others see more purpose for themselves in whatever life is left for them. The "why go on?" question would come up repeatedly if the loss was a close significant other (such as a spouse or child) and no sense could be made of the immediate loss of life. Obviously, the relationship also dictates the time and trajectory of the emptiness felt. For Kevin, who lost his only brother, Mark, aged sixty-two, to COVID-19, it was instantaneous.

There was an immediate sense of emptiness upon learning of my brother's death, almost as if a part of me was now missing. We shared so much of life together. Every other day, it seemed, we shared texts of photos of our grandchildren as well as photos of wildlife, as we both found such joy in them. We spoke weekly by phone. I was crushed as I thought about our plans for trips to our northern seasonal cabin where we hunted and fished annually. I couldn't imagine all these experiences without him. This empty feeling reoccurred every time I traveled up to the cabin, every time I walked to the river and went out into the woods. It was all just gone.

The emptiness seeped in quietly at times, and at other times it came in like a tidal wave in that first year. In the second year, the processing of these memories went from an emptiness to a sense of frustration and even anger.

Kevin's grief journey started with emptiness and moved into strong emotions of anger and frustration, which were then worked through in an instrumental sort of way. He began to incorporate reminders of Mark's unique personality into the northern cabin landscape, which helped him to create legacy and a connecting bond with his brother. The relationship bond continued but moved from the physical to the spiritual realm. One beautiful gesture was when he renamed the Upper Peninsula of Michigan hunting cabin by constructing a wood sign and placing it at the front door; "Mark's Place," it now proudly displays.

Feelings of emptiness and surrender take on different forms for all of us. Some bereaved individuals refer to the emptiness as though they were numb and just walking around without a sense of direction, a *going-through-the-motions* kind of feeling. While still others may experience it after a long and dreary wrestling with the grief over an extended period.

It is not an easy task to be fully present after a significant loss. With compassion for oneself, in due course the sadness, anger, and other feelings will continue to emerge but then start to melt away. Dr. Tara Brach, a psychologist, suggests that

> in the groundless openness of sorrow, there is a wholeness of presence and a deep natural wisdom.... Even in the midst of our deepest emotional suffering, self-compassion is the pathway that will carry us home.

Eventually, with mindfulness, a calm environment, distance from disruptive forces, and other self-care practices, my peace came back, and the way forward became clearer.

Quiet time practices

Exercises that can help to quiet the mind with these intense feelings include practices such as mindfulness and centered prayer. It can be quite challenging during sorrowful times brought on by overwhelming grief, which is why I encourage people to incorporate these exercises into a daily routine long before they need them.

Mindfulness has become quite popular and is the ability to be fully present in one's surroundings and movements, which brings forth a deep awareness of *being* and helps us to be more in tune with thoughts and feelings. One goal of this practice is to arouse our inner workings related to our physical, emotional, and mental processes. Becoming aware of one's breathing, for example, will help to rein in these intense feelings and bring a sense of calm and peace. Although we cannot be fully present in each moment of every waking hour, this practice does help us to experience life in a new way as we quiet the mind.

When working through memories of the deceased, we often encounter various reminders of them. There are many objects, such as photos and personal belongings or gifts to us, as well as sounds (favorite music) and smells that can often trigger these memories. It is also normal to think about what could have been, the memories unmade. When these times overwhelm us with high emotion, a quiet time practice is very beneficial to have in one's self-care tool kit.

There are numerous phone apps and YouTube videos to help learn to incorporate the practice of mindfulness. I prefer to use *Centering Prayer*, an app provided free from Contemplative Outreach. The app is designed to be a receptive method of Christian silent prayer where the aim is to assist us in deepening our relationship with God:

> The indwelling Presence...a prayer in which we can experience God's presence within us, closer than breathing, closer than thinking, closer than consciousness itself.

This app allows for one to choose from lists of opening and closing prayers along with sounds of musical instruments. So you custom-build your experience and can change it daily, weekly, or not at all. It has aided me in becoming more aware of my breathing and thought processes and created the perfect platform for quietness. It is a technique of silent prayer that enables us to receive the gift of contemplative prayer. It is a form of prayer that is a discipline to foster our relationship with God (Centering Prayer, Google Play Apps; Fathers Thomas Keating, William Meninger, and Basil Pennington).

There are four guidelines to this type of centering prayer. First, you choose a sacred word as a symbol of your intention to consent to the presence of God and action within. Next, as you sit comfortably with closed eyes, you focus on the sacred word choice. After a short engagement with your thoughts (which include body sensations, feelings, images, and reflections), you return gently to the sacred word. Lastly, you remain in silence with closed eyes for an amount of time you set beforehand. You choose from selections of music for a beginning sound, the amount of time you want for your silent duration, an ending sound, and then a closing prayer. This particular phone app is made possible by *Contemplative Outreach*, which is a spiritual network of individuals and small faith communities who are committed to living the contemplative dimension of the gospel of Christ.

Mindfulness practices have been gaining in popularity for some time now and can be done anywhere at any time. It involves an ability to be fully present in the moment without becoming overly reactive or overwhelmed by whatever is happening around us. Mindfulness can wake up the inner workings of our mental, emotional, and physical processes and result in a more peaceful existence. It is a practice to work toward. It is an ideal to move nearer to. Again, a reminder that one cannot sustain being fully present in every moment, however, as we are distracted with the tasks of living and doing.

Another helpful exercise is quick calm breathing, which is easy to learn and a handy tool to assist with panic attacks, for example, often brought on by a clashing of emotions triggered by unexpected reminders of the death. I use it regularly when I feel anxious to promote relaxation. It connects the body and the mind in a way that brings calm as hormones are released onto the vagus nerve and the tension melts away.

I recall a story when this was helpful in the caregiving of an older parent. My father was taken by ambulance to the emergency room of a local hospital, and I followed by car. When I arrived, a physician was ordering numerous tests that my dad had recently been through. I approached and asked if they could contact his physician's office and see if the results of these tests were in his medical records. I desired for them to be accessed so we did not have to put him through more agony when he was obviously struggling. The physician was not open to this and proceeded forward.

I left the emergency room to go move my vehicle and call Mom with an update. I felt distressed that at ninety years old, he had to go through so much. Dad had so much fear in his eyes, and I wanted to diminish his suffering. I reached out to a support person by text and told her in brief what I was dealing with. "At ER with Dad, frustrating!" Being a wise woman and social work professional, she texted back one word: *Breathe!* Although simple advice, this was truly helpful as I remembered my quick calm breathing exercise and practiced it after I parked the car. I had been distracted with the circumstances, and as a result, the rhythm of my breathing was not in sync. I sat with the realization, for a few minutes, that Dad's body was failing him, and all I could do was to be his advocate, but I needed to be still and calm. I was processing loss as I watched the decline of my father and felt a bit helpless. As I reentered the hospital setting, I was much calmer and confident in advocating for Dad. I remember telling the nurse that "Perhaps Dr. Smith was insulted that I may have questioned his authority and reasoning," to which he quickly replied, "Oh no! That's his everyday 'I'm in charge' attitude." *Yikes*, I thought, *these poor patients.*

Sitting with the grief can be a blessing if we allow the anguish to transform us into better human beings. But that takes self-compassion and patience. It means moving away from the ego. Again, Brooks, in his book *The Second Mountain,* does a splendid job of explaining how to accomplish this, how to be other-centered and to desire the things that are truly worth wanting. Using a sociological lens, he describes "second mountain people" as those who went through a deep valley of suffering and then they rise up. They surrender to a life commitment and embrace a life of interdependence, not independence as the culture prescribes. I cannot help but add "autonomy is overrated."

Suffering can teach us to live life more deeply. If we remain open and positive, it has the potential to lead us right into an awakening for deep contemplation, which requires silence. The Venerable Fulton J. Sheen (1895–1979), a renowned theologian and American bishop in the Catholic Church, suggests that "prayer begins by talking to God, but it ends by listening to him. In the face of absolute truth, silence is the soul's language." It is in the silence that we connect with our Creator and gain strength and peace.

As I moved deeper into this period of stillness, it seemed to free me from the expectations of myself and others and allowed for a turning point. I asked myself, What has this chapter in life taught me? I was gradually pulled toward solitude. I suddenly desired to be alone (a move toward introversion [Rohr, p. 144]) to ponder what grief, loss, and suffering were teaching me. Although I wanted to answer the whys, the hows, and the what ifs, a strong urge to be still and to just be present in my environment was persistent.

My hope was in a renewal of my spirit for the tasks in life remaining. I knew this period was spiritual in nature and that I had to step back, let go, and surrender to the stillness, to get some relief from the painful aching of the heart. At the same time, I knew not to be hard on myself for all the grieving to date, as it only reflected my love for the lost relationships and the appreciation I had for my niece, my cousin's husband, my mother, and my brother-in-law. I was grateful to have been the aunt, the cousin, the daughter, and the sister-in-law to those who are now gone.

It seems equally important to discuss allowing for a time of "open space" where we can use our imagination, our wonder, and our creativity as we anticipate our new future without the deceased. This can include processing our grief through art or music. We don't always have to use words to construct a story. There are numerous resources for addressing this including workshops and retreats designed specifically around challenging times in life, which can help people to express their emotions surrounding a grief experience. They might include the use of painting, wood carving, photography, and so forth.

Experiencing the divine

As the world continued to spin out of control with the pandemic while we carried our grief, a need for a quieter existence grew, one without all the debates and conversations on world events that seemed to be going nowhere. I craved being in nature and at the lake, to listen to the waves, walk the beach, talk with God, and savor the quiet stillness of the rural area. I found myself moving away from an empty space to a place of deep, reflective thought in order to experience the divine. I recalled a book I read in my early adult years where the author focused on the importance of reflection and its meanings:

> Reflection has many meanings. It has to do with the wonderful world around us no less than with the world within. In each case we are asked to look once more into the soul of things, including the soul of self. When we do, when we catch hold of a realization that there is always something hidden, always something yet to be discovered, always goals beyond our goals, and meanings beyond the obvious-then, for a little while, life becomes transformed. (M. Bach 1965, p. 18)

I wanted so much for these losses to be transformative, and it was through this period of inner quiet that I was able to experience the changes going on in myself. God's love was experienced deep in my soul. I stopped searching and questioning and started listening. And I knew every step was necessary, so none of it was viewed as a waste of time and energy.

All through this grief journey, I was watching for signs of connection, or what we call "extraordinary experiences" in the field of bereavement study, from those we lost. As believers in an afterlife, these experiences often bring us hope that those we lost are in a heavenly realm not far away.

Through the work of Dr. Louis E. LaGrand, who is a leader in the field of grief counseling, we learn that these are common experiences that the bereaved report. They often bring comfort and reassurance in a time of great sorrow. Dr. LaGrand wrote a wonderful book, *Love Lives On: Learning from the Extraordinary Encounters of the Bereaved,* which has been well received.

These signs for us came in different forms for me and others noted in these stories of loss. After my brother died, there were bright, shiny pennies that would show up out of nowhere. They always brought a smile to my face and gave me a sense that he was still with us, only now in spirit.

My husband has had the same experience, especially in times of distress. On the last day of working for a company and losing his job because of an unexpected health concern, he was cleaning out his delivery truck and was overwhelmed with sadness at this abrupt ending. As he finished and went to shut the driver's door, a bright, shiny penny was centered on a car mat he had already cleaned. He snatched it up, smiled, and flipped it in the air saying, "Thanks, Jerry, I needed that!" as he moved on. He brought the shiny penny home and excitedly shared the story as a reminder that "all would be well," a message he felt was being delivered from a brother-in-law of over forty years whom he loved and missed. We have many more of these stories that we believe connect us closely to an exceptional experience of the divine in memory of the deceased.

My brother Jeff shares how strongly they feel the spirit of their daughter as they grieve her loss in their family:

> Anna had thick, long hair, and each day my wife would make it look perfect with a small hair band to keep it in a ponytail. A simple small hair band. Since she has been gone, we seem to find hair bands everywhere. In grocery store parking lots, at work, on sidewalks, wherever we go, we find them. We probably have found 30–40 of them in the last 2-plus years. A sign from Anna, we are certain of that.

In a large research study with the widowed, I had numerous participants who wanted to see what I thought about an "experience" they had, yet they did not feel comfortable bringing these up in their grief support groups. I was an objective stranger, and they knew I was well versed in bereavement research. When I shut off the recorder at the end of their interviews, I gave them a list of written grief resources in their area and asked if they had any questions for me. The stories of extraordinary experiences that followed, and they entrusted me with, were comforting to them. I saw no harm in their belief that the deceased might be sending them their way. They wanted to tell someone. And yet they feared family members, close friends, and even grief support group facilitators might think that they had lost it somehow from believing this might be coming from their deceased spouse.

These signs are not always experienced by all and can also cause distress to those who do not encounter them. I have had comments of concern about why only certain people in the family are getting these messages, and I have no answer for that. "Stay hopeful," I tell the bereaved.

Each of us has our own unfolding of the disconnect of a physical relationship with someone loved and will have a new and possibly even deeper bond after death. My advice is to contemplate the unexpected and focus on what that person loved in life and then carry their legacy forward, all the while being at peace about developing your own legacy in your remaining days. Let the experiences of death and loss of someone loved be teachable chapters in life on how to appreciate and cherish life itself.

Key takeaways

> Recognize and name the strong emotions.
> Lean into the pain (experience it).
> Push the pause button.
> Find balance with emotions and tasks.
> Identify what inhibits your ability to be still.
> Practice mindfulness and/or centering prayer.
> Sit with the "not knowing."
> Surrender.
> Let emptiness bring peace.
> Practice self-compassion.
> Identify and lean on strong support persons.
> Stay open to extraordinary experiences.

CHAPTER 6

Transition/Transformation/ Perspective

I have learned along my own grief journey how important it is to allow time to self-reflect in order to see the impact of the experience in my life. To arrive at an answer, I had to be honest with myself. Starting with an examination of my values and transitioning to identifying just what anchors me in life were the first steps toward transformational thinking.

I spoke to family members at various points as they processed their losses, and what I recognized was that a liminal state surfaced for us all, just not in the same way or at the same time.

Liminal state

A liminal state refers to a place people find themselves in during a transitional period. It can be a physical gap (such as a doorway), an emotional one (such as when one is in the midst of a grief narrative) or metaphorical (a decision to be made). I like to call it the "in-between space." For example, this emerges when a caregiver no longer has the ill and/or disabled person to provide care for because they have been placed in a facility or they have died. Maureen, who lost her daughter suddenly, explains where she is in this transition from her caregiver role in the "before times" to her life now in the "after times" after nearly three years.

> I am working my overnight shift at a major retailer. I sort the boxes of apparel and accessories as they come off the truck. It's a solitary job. I like that. As I am performing my mundane tasks, I sometimes feel an out-of-body experience where I'm an observer looking down on the other me. I ask myself, "How the hell did I get here? Why am I acting as if this is normal? What happened to my life???" In February 2020, in one instant, shocking moment my life changed. My daughter, the love of my life, my soulmate, was gone. And everything was different.
>
> I had spent the bulk of my adult life as a caregiver for my precious girl. Her needs consumed my days and nights, but her radiant, pure, beautiful spirit filled my heart. Literally everything I did revolved around her needs. It was exhausting, yes, but the joy I got from her presence greatly outweighed any negatives. And then it was gone. She was gone. And I had nothing. Nothing.
>
> I had begun running when my daughter was young. I did it so I could stay healthy for her and for the mental benefits it offered. I was able to lift, transfer and carry her even though she weighed more than I did. I never needed in-home assistance from anyone. And I liked it that way. I was strong and powerful. I was a fierce

mama bear. Now I am none of those things. I tried to continue running, but flashbacks and lack of motivation interfere.

I was fierce and fearless in the before times. Now I am afraid to go out, dreading seeing neighbors and friends. What do I say when they ask how I'm doing? I hate acting "normal" around my co-workers, most of whom don't know my story. I feel like a fraud, a bad actor. I miss the people who worked at my daughter's day program. I miss her doctors and nurses. They loved her almost as much as I did. But time moves on, and they have other responsibilities.

So here I am in the "after times." It feels as if I have opened a portal into an alternate universe, and I can't get out of it. I am trapped in a world I hate, and I don't understand. I have become an actor playing the part of myself. And I'm really bad at it.

I believe that this liminal state holds such great uncertainty and unpredictability. This place often signifies an ending of one role that we filled and the beginning of another in one's own life. For some, it is a lonely and emotionally demanding place and often not an enjoyable one because it takes work. And when you are exhausted from the grief, you have little energy to construct any new role. Or when the world is shut down as it was in Maureen's initial grief period, it is hard to even begin to start a new future and work on a new identity. However, it can also be valuable and transformative in providing us with the prospect to move forward into a new period in our lives.

One's identity is often in sharp focus when liminality arrives. Herein lies the paradox of liminal space because, on one hand, you feel uncomfortable and uncertain (the ending of a role you may have had for years), and on the other, there is a chance to learn and grow and watch a new part of your life emerge (the new beginning, although oftentimes an unwanted one). Let's look at how Maureen describes "what's next" in her life as she approaches year three of her bereavement:

> I wish I could see a future where I can carry the weight of losing my soulmate/best friend/child and transform it into loving memory instead of crushing sadness. It hasn't happened yet. Not even close. I do have moments of fleeting happiness. Not everything is gloom and doom. I have a large and supportive family. I live in a beautiful part of the country. My son is engaged to a young woman who I will be proud to call my daughter-in-law. I have a new, energetic Lab puppy. All of those are good things. I get that. But they will never ultimately replace or outweigh the crushing sadness. There have been a few well-meaning people who have assured me that I will find my passion. I thank them, but I know it's not true. I already lived that. Even if I were interested in a new career or cause, I live with terrible brain fog (grief fog?) and social anxiety.
>
> So at least for now I will live my life in survival mode. Just get through each day. Let numbness take over when it is needed. Acknowledge the small victories. But I no longer can summon the forced optimism I used to practice. I just hope that there is a loving God who will one day reunite me with my daughter. I guess that will have to be my passion for now.

In some sense, Maureen has transitioned to her new life without her daughter, although it was a forced transition. She has somewhat of a new identity in her role at her job. Although, as she describes it, "as a bad actor," it's still a new role, and she is functioning in it. She has hope for a future for her son and his soon-to-be wife. And then, there's the new Lab puppy, and she is "caring" for her now. This transition took some time to arrive at and adjust to, but nonetheless, it has begun.

Another example of transitory space was evident with cousin Debra as she moved from her past identity of being Mrs. Wade Edward to the now new widowed state. This new label was assigned suddenly but took time to adjust to. At the two-and-a-half-year mark after the death of her husband of twenty-three years, Debra tells us:

> I still go back and forth between the two roles. What I mean by that is that I really hate having to take on the role that my husband had. He took care of all the maintenance for both our home and our cottage, and I never gave it much thought, until his diagnosis. Now that I have the sole responsibility for running both households and maintaining them, I find it very challenging. It is exhausting on top of the extra worry about the economy, which is problematic with the expense of two houses. I cannot spend the money like I had thought.
>
> There is no way around it. He took on most of the male-dominated tasks, and I do not know how to do any of that, so I have to hire most of it done. I am realizing that you can't go on and take on both roles at an older age. I am older now. I want less responsibility and tasks, not more. At 70, why should I learn how to operate the riding lawn mower?
>
> At first, there was an expectation it seemed by everyone that I would just assume the role, but then you realize you don't necessarily want to. A lot of it goes back to my childhood as my dad, a Merchant Marine, left to go work on the Great Lakes freighter boats for 9 months out of the year. I was 7, and we had to assume the maintenance role to help our mother (my brother, sister and I).

It all came flashing back, that childhood chapter in my life. I did not want that role either, but it fell in our laps, and you do what you should do for your parents. My mother could not assume the maintenance role and did not want to anyway, but my parents had a rather modest income, so she could not afford to hire everything done, such as the lawn cutting.

Everyone assumes that if you have money, which I do, you will be fine, but this is not the case. Try finding a consistent all-around handyman like I have had to do. My husband was built-in. He would say, you must learn how to run this snowblower, but I remember saying, "Really?" And then not learning how. Neither one of us really looked too far ahead to old age, especially after his diagnosis. When the Lewy body dementia diagnosis arrived, it was mild at the beginning, so he kept trying to fix and maintain things as he had always done because he was stubborn and didn't want anyone else fixing anything. But, as time moved on, he made things worse. He attempted to repair equipment by taking it all apart and then not remembering how it went back together, so it seemed as though nothing worked by the time he died.

Over the eight years of his illness, both households went downhill, and so now, I have been faced with many projects and repairs. With Covid-19 the year he died and now this economic shift, it has made everything a very challenging new role to transition into, that of "widow." There was not just an unsettling feeling in my personal life, but in our whole world. At the same time as my husband was at the end of his illness, the world began to crumble and is currently in

> more dangerous territory it seems as we approach 2024 elections. I have moments of great joy as I strive to look at all I have and be grateful, yet I then see the uncertainty staring us all in our faces and experience deep sadness.
>
> How can I cultivate more peacefulness? I may have to look back on good times and then look forward with a more hopeful perspective for better days ahead.

Transitioning into new roles when the world is not certain is doubly hard as Debra attests. She associates her current responsibilities due to having to take on her deceased's husbands' role to that of what she had in her childhood. She speaks as though there was no choice then, and she was frustrated at times by having extra responsibilities growing up. And now, she is in a similar situation, one she does not like or want. Rather, she had hoped to be enjoying more of "what was left of her life." To some extent, she is able to do this now that the virus is less threatening and she is vaccinated and boosted, but the rate of inflation has made her pause. She wonders if her money will hold out as she had anticipated. It seemed to consume her thoughts more and more as the cost of living climbs. These ongoing concerns point to the restoration-oriented tasks that need attention as we process loss and change.

In the last line of her quoted excerpt above, she asks herself, "How can I cultivate more peacefulness?" After honoring her struggles and challenges, I encouraged her to think more about the good times and moments both present and past in order to shift her mindset. I asked her to consider the moments that made her smile or those that gave her pause.

Moments of awe

People tend to describe words quite differently depending on their experiences. Awe can be defined as an emotion, a response to stimuli. Through this writing, I have learned just how varied these descriptions of awe moments are. I like to think of them as those times when something or someone is so beautiful that it takes my breath away. I don't mean beautiful in the physical sense but rather in acts of kindness to others or in profound words and stories.

There are often moments that provide me with a strong sense of being anointed spiritually from a higher power when they are occurring. They can be accompanied at times with actual goose bumps! When a child reminds me of an old soul and says something enlightened beyond their years, I am in awe. These times give me hope, often ease my mind, and lighten my often too serious mood.

When I think of the accumulated losses, there have been awe moments that have presented us with a sense of wonderment. They surprise us, give us pause, and spark a confidence in solidifying a belief in an afterlife. Sometimes, they come through the finding of objects that the deceased had a liking to, moments in nature connected to the memory of the deceased (an eagle), or favorite music, and there have been many.

As noted earlier, ever since I lost my brother Jeremiah, I find bright, shiny pennies, often in times of distress. He loved to play the lottery even though he was well-off financially from all his hard work over his lifetime. Upon finding these coins, we have an immediate sense of his presence, almost as if he is watching over us. Other family members have told similar stories; see *Experiencing the divine* section in chapter 5.

Recently, as I was traveling to speak to a group of bereaved individuals at my mother's church, an hour's drive from my home, I decided to pray the rosary she had given me. I keep it in my car on the rearview mirror. I took it down, connected my rosary app to the car's Bluetooth and drove off. However, instead of the rosary app narrator, the media connected to my music playlist. This list has literally hundreds of songs. It pulled up "Lord, I Hope This Day Is Good" by Don Williams, the very song played and sung by our paternal cousins at my mother's gravesite on her day of burial. It was a moment of pure awe. I was stunned! I felt as though either she, or God, was very close.

Unfortunately, most bereaved people do not feel comfortable sharing these stories for fear the recipient will think they have gone off the deep end. I, too, find myself reserving these stories for people I know for certain believe in an afterlife. (And here they are now for the world to see!)

I recall a story my husband, Kevin, bereaved of his younger brother, recently shared about how many times he was seeing an eagle in the skies above him at the northern hunting cabin. Each time he did, he thought of his brother, Mark, who loved birds. On a northern trip to the cabin that both Mark and Kevin loved, a mutual friend had joined them. He, too, was a good friend to Mark in his lifetime. As he was fishing at a spot where Mark loved to fish, an eagle flew in and was close enough to lock eyes with him. It was a moment that will never be forgotten. In over fifty years of spending time at this northern treasure, Kevin notes that they have never seen an eagle flying above. This friend exclaimed to Kevin, "I don't consider myself a believer, but if that's not a sign of Mark's presence, nothing is."

Some have questioned, Is it the one who died sending us these bright spots, or are they from God who now sees our pain and need for hope as we grieve? We cannot be sure. What I do know for certain is that they comfort people and bring hope, which has the capacity to give us a new perspective.

Adopting a new perspective

For a short while after each of our losses, it was hard to see anything but the pain and sorrow as we felt the absence so keenly of the ones we loved. Then, the frustration. But several of us realized quite early on that we needed to shift our perspective to save ourselves from a long and lonely road of gloomy grief. We did not deny our feelings and emotions, but we also knew that we had to look deeply into each loss, practice compassion, and count our blessings if we wanted to survive the aching hearts. For those like me, grieving as a relative and not a chief mourner, it was obviously a quicker transition because the loss did not impact me on the same level as a grieving mother or wife.

We had always practiced this shift in perspective with our children as they grew. If they had a bad day at school or a friend was mean to them, we would help them to explore other avenues rather than focus for too long on the obvious, their own hurt feelings. "Perhaps the little guy who kicked you had some harm done to him recently? Let's try to be thankful that this did not escalate into a much worse scenario."

The better route to take is the one of gratitude, kindness, and exploration. What has this incident or experience taught us? We all can benefit from more truth and goodness. If we only look at our problems (and our losses) as difficult and painful, we will react in a way that keeps us from living life in a hopeful way forward.

If we can teach our children to find compassion when mistreated, then we can apply this to our circumstances when we might feel as though the death we are grieving is unwarranted or untimely or simply just not fair. This is not always as easy as it sounds and often takes much longer for some of us, depending on the relationship lost and the circumstances around it. Practicing a positive perspective can help.

Gratitude

I believe we are not inclined to be immediately thankful during the processing of a loss that was unexpected or traumatic in nature, but we can arrive there in time. If we look closely, we can find ways to be grateful for moments and people who made the path just a little lighter. Of course, the circumstances of the death are a factor in the timeline of when we can recognize the benefits of being grateful. When someone we love is murdered or if the person died by suicide, for example, it will take a great deal of patience and time to uncover any good that may come out of these situations.

After brother Mark died of COVID-19, it was hard to think we might find some benefit. He was well loved, needed in his family, and had much life yet to live. Yet as we reflected, we knew to be grateful that his priest was able to be with him in his last moments, anoint him, and pray with him. We were grateful that his wife was able to see him in person toward the end of his life. And in the immediate and difficult initial grief, we were grateful that his parents had gone before him as it would have crushed them.

Another example might be the frustration and agony that can arrive when there is dysfunction in the family unit. Regardless of the reason for the disputes, whether that be values, personalities, or the unattended grief, for example, we must attempt to do the right thing for the person in our care. We may have to learn to dance with others while emotions are high, but in so doing, we must honor the wishes of the dying at the same time. It takes self-control and, in many instances, self-awareness of what we are doing and saying and what we have failed to do or say.

There is often a good deal of anticipatory grief in circumstances where we see the frail and failing loved one fading away. People are imagining and anticipating what is to come and oftentimes unaware of how it is impacting their interactions within the family unit. Changing how we look at it as it unfolds, from disgust for those creating the conflict to compassion for their hurting hearts or their need for power, often helps us to finish strong in challenging circumstances. This often involves forgiveness on some level. Oprah's quote on forgiveness is a great help once we are able move away from the situation, which can take years depending on the damage, and consider what the pain has taught us: "True forgiveness is when you can say: Thank you for that experience." The pain reminds us and teaches us "how not to be" toward others who are in challenging circumstances.

Arriving at a place where we saw some goodness from the pain allowed for a shift in how we processed the loss. It ultimately enabled us to move forward in adapting to our new role in life (which includes identity work) and to give back in similar situations. The compiling of excerpts from our stories and the writing of this book are part of our contribution to helping others. I recall the words of former *President Barack Obama*, which seem appropriate here:

> The best way to not feel hopeless is to get
> up and do something. Don't wait for good things

to happen to you. If you go out and make some good things happen, you will fill the world with hope, you will fill yourself with hope.

Not everyone has the same timeline and capacity as this book has shown throughout, so self-compassion is warranted.

Self-Compassion

Learning to be more compassionate with ourselves in our grief is a practice I cannot emphasize enough. Being kind to others who are suffering comes naturally to most of us; however, we may not even recognize how much we ignore our own needs. Dr. Kristin Neff, an educational psychologist, reminds us of the many myths related to self-compassion, that we mistakenly think it is the same as self-pity; that it will lead to weakness; make us lazy; that we will become more narcissistic, and it is too self-centered. The opposite is true. We will become more emotionally stable as a result of practicing self-compassion.

This approach of self-compassion has the capacity to protect us from mental health ailments, such as anxiety, which will wreak havoc over time and needs our attention. It will certainly help us to become better at caring for others. We can apply this as a self-care tool as we sort through loss. Using Dr. Neff's application, by practicing being kind to ourselves as we move through the grief, we honor our own humanness.

In order to unconditionally love anyone, we must first love and care for ourselves. As we have learned from previous chapters, using practices such as mindfulness, centering prayer, or sitting with not knowing the answers to our questions all move us in the direction of self-compassion. We are each here for a purpose, and we can only arrive at that purpose if we look in the mirror first and love our imperfections and humanness. Only then can we truly love our neighbor.

With our multiple losses, there was a good deal of dislike for ourselves in the form of regret and guilt, yet these were unreasonable criticisms as we had forces out of our control, namely COVID-19 restrictions. We learned to acknowledge these feelings as they are common but then to let go of our disappointments surrounding some of these circumstances (i.e., inability to be present at the death-bed, to have a full ritual and/or funeral services, etc.). Eventually, we began to focus more on how we could examine our new role without the deceased, make connections with others, and help them at the same time.

Key takeaways

Self-reflect on what this loss is teaching you.

Loss transitions often include uncertainty as one role ends (i.e., caregiver, spouse, parent, etc.).

Current world conditions make transitions, transformation, and adopting a healthy new perspective more challenging.

Look for "awe moments."

Shift your perspective from negative to positive.

Cultivate gratitude.

Be compassionate toward yourself.

PART III

Courage

CHAPTER 7

Identity Work/Connection/ Helping Others

....

Our prime purpose in this life is to help others. And if
you can't help them, at least don't hurt them.

—Dalai Lama

....

Constructing a new identity

Many bereaved individuals are unable, at least initially, to recognize that they are adjusting to a new role. With spousal loss, for example, this may require the newly bereaved to take on all the tasks that the person who died once held responsibility for (maintenance, financial matters, etc.). It could also result from an adjustment back to a previous state, where one is no longer a caregiver (such as an adult child who provided care for a parent, a parent who took care of a child, etc.). The self becomes fractured when loss occurs, and self-reflection is necessary with questions and exploration. For example, asking "Who am I now? I am not Mrs. John Smith. I am a widow, and I've never been a widow, so how do I do this?" Moving through grief may involve examining the temporal aspects of one's identity.

When my mother died, I was no longer a caregiver after five years of learning to be one. Both my parents were now deceased, and I remember thinking, *Am I no longer a daughter either?* Our roles take time to learn and unlearn. It is good to be patient in the process and use self-compassion. This is especially evident with the widowed population. Regardless of age, many of them do not want the new label of widow or widower and feel a great deal of frustration around the tasks and responsibilities they now have in addition to the work of grief.

Coming up from the valley

Typically, bereaved individuals have been focused on just putting one foot in front of the other for a very long time. Often, they ask me, How can I possibly provide any help to another right now when I can barely function from the crippling grief? Instinctively, people know when they can pull themselves out enough to lend a hand to lessen the suffering of others. But our help to others can be spread just from deciding to do the simple things. Smiling at a stranger when we are hurting can lift us as well as the other. Attending a support group and offering a strategy that helped you in your initial grief just might assist another newer member who is struggling. Mutual help has been proven to be liberating for all parties.

I remember a story from years ago when I was attempting to accept the loss of a child by miscarriage. My pastor at the time asked me (3 months into dealing with our loss) to go visit a mother who had lost a child full-term. I initially cringed as I compared my pain to what hers must be like, and it was unimaginable to me to think of losing a new infant versus a child in utero. So I was comparing our grief journeys and trying to escape the encounter.

I honestly also had become quite comfortable in my own valley of suffering and had settled into it. Although I did not feel up to it, my pastor persisted, and I reluctantly agreed. The young mother made a connection with me, a stranger, immediately. She shared all her shattered hopes and dreams for the child she never brought home from the hospital. There was a lock of his hair, his footprint mold, the outfit she had planned to bring him home in. She talked and cried with me for over an hour. She thanked me for visiting and asked about my miscarriage and listened intently to every detail.

The visit gave meaning to my pain when I had such a warm response from this bereaved mother. I still grieved my loss but also knew that I had something of value to share with others who were suffering a similar experience as I saw her grief lifted as well. We saw one another a few more times and shared resources (helpful books, such as *Empty Arms: Emotional Support for Those Who Have Suffered Miscarriage or Stillbirth* by Vredevelt, given to me by a dear friend from Ohio). I was so grateful to this bereaved new mom and to the pastor who knew the value of mutual help. This visit with her pulled me up and out of the valley that I had fallen into and one that would have likely led to much more long-suffering.

As newly bereaved young mothers, we both began to realize that there were others who might benefit from sharing experiences of the loss of a child. I learned through this experience that on some level, reaching out and helping her meant I was living forward. Both my shared story and expressed pain were meaningful to her.

As I look back on that time of great sorrow, I am encouraged as I recall the words of Pope Francis:

> Rivers do not drink their own water; trees do not eat their own fruit; the sun does not shine on itself and flowers do not spread their fragrance for themselves. Living for others is a rule of nature. We are born to help each other. No matter how difficult it is. Life is good when you are happy but much better when others are happy because of you. Let us remember that pain is a sign that we are alive, problems are a sign that we are strong and prayer is a sign that we are not alone. If we can acknowledge these truths and condition our hearts and minds, our lives will

be more meaningful, different and worthwhile."
(Pope Francis 2020).

There is also a great body of research making a connection between our own happiness that comes from helping others. Dr. Sonja Lyubomirsky, a professor of psychology at the University of California, Riverside, along with her colleague (J. Kurtz and S. Lyubomirsky 2008), found that performing acts of kindness had long lasting changes in a person's well-being. She built on research by Piliavin (2003), who suggests that prosocial behavior has positive outcomes for both the giver and the receiver. She writes with many colleagues who found that happy people cope more effectively with stress in their lives, have stronger immune systems, and may even live longer (Fredrickson 2001; Lyubomirsky, King, and Diener 2005).

I have learned from the pain of loss that my life is more meaningful because of empathic others who have been on the journey with me in this collective human race. I am grateful that they had the courage to support me as I attempted to bring some meaning to my distress.

Making sense of the suffering

I remember attending a funeral for an elderly gentleman who had suffered for over five years from cancer and was cared for in his home by his wife of forty-two years. The new widow was exhausted at the funeral visitation. She kept sighing and finally turned to me (while looking over at her husband's body lying in his casket), saying, "There is a shifting now from his physical pain and suffering to my emotional suffering from losing him." It was if, at that moment, she realized, with great resignation, that she must embrace the suffering as her ongoing companion. She told me she had made sense of the suffering through her belief system. It is one that taught her that, as humans, we will all suffer in some way, as it is part of the human condition. Some of us can easily accept what comes with illness and death and the grief that ensues, but many who experience tragic or sudden death, the death of a young person, or a meaningless violent death often have a longer road to travel. Making sense out of these types of circumstances and coming to a place of resignation and peace will take patience and time. But I am convinced that with a good support circle of people who understand loss and a strong faith, we can persevere.

I believe we try out ideas with people on making sense of what has happened in a death that seemingly has no meaning to us. We construct our story in a way that we can easily edit it if it is not well received, especially if it is from violence or a death that goes against the natural law, such as the death of a child. Making some sense out of why the deceased may have suffered and now why the bereaved family has to suffer can take years or even a lifetime. The construction of their story of loss may seem too painful to speak of or even to put together. As noted in earlier chapters, one may have to sit with the "not knowing" as there are no answers to some of our questions, which means there is no sense to be made of it all. The only hope for some may come in the way of connection with others who suffer a similar heartache.

Connection brings solace

Solace arrives when we find someone with a similar story whose pain is hard to make sense of as well. This is why support groups for the bereaved are so helpful as people listen to the stories of others and can relate to the pain, which reminds them that they are not alone. They see up close that others are getting through it and are not "going crazy." Some of the more seasoned members of the group (in terms of how far along they are in the grief journey) offer strategies and advice. I have been told that this expressed generosity takes them out of their own pain.

Many groups that once met face-to-face are now still meeting in online venues that have some value at 3:00 a.m. when someone cannot sleep and needs connection. Organized in-person support groups are not for everyone. Some people prefer keeping their grief private and may have strong and ample support, but for those who do not, the support group is often a lifesaver for the long journey.

Riding the emotional roller coaster of grief over and over is exhausting. It impacts every part of our being, and the emotional suffering can be quite intense. Good support is critical. When people who knew the deceased check in on you, it brings a connectedness that is often welcomed and reinforces that the life of the person lost had value and meaning. However, most of the working through of grief is done in private. This can quickly lead to isolation and loneliness, which can be dangerous for some and was certainly reflective in our lockdowns during the pandemic. A great loneliness naturally often accompanies the suffering as mom Maureen attests:

> Grief has been described as a "seething loneliness." A character in a recent television show said of life after loss, "After a while you learn to live with the unacceptable." For me it has been both. Every day I try to summon the strength to crawl out of the massive hole that is my pain. Some days I feel like I am making progress. Some days Grief kicks me in the head, and I fall back to the bottom of that hole. Will I ever conquer that challenge and emerge at the top? I guess I will just have to keep trying.

Maureen prefers to keep her grief private except for sharing feelings and stories with select family members through texting, and that connection, she notes, "has saved her." In some bereavements, there is little to no energy for a very long period to "help others" as Maureen explained through her struggles with daily life tasks and the ebb and flow of the grief roller coaster. She is living forward, however, at her own pace, in her own time, and that is being respected by these select family members. For those living in her home, it requires more patience than from those who are not impacted in person. As some move forward and others do not, life brings yet more challenges.

Shared humanity

I firmly believe that in order to appreciate a shared humanity, we must all respect each other's inherent dignity. Many people, regardless of their spiritual beliefs, accept as true that we benefit from recognizing and honoring the dignity each of us deserves. Brooks reminds us that "the soul is the piece of us that gives each person infinite dignity and worth." The sermon excerpt shared earlier on suffering from Fr. Joe also attests to the importance of protecting our dignity. In our shared humanity, respect is essential.

The work of Dr. Donna Hicks, an expert on this subject of dignity, provides us with vital elements for this concept. She writes:

> Our shared desire for dignity transcends all our differences…putting our common human identity above all else.

Included in the essential elements on this topic is the ability for acknowledgment of each other. We all want to be respected by being seen, heard, and understood. This is especially true when we are grieving a significant loss, when we suffer, and when conflict needs a resolution. We want our pain recognized and our stories witnessed without judgment, as this helps us to make sense out of the suffering we endure and to feel as though others care.

Some form of connection with others, whether these are other bereaved individuals or not, is important. Grief is isolating, and sometimes we can get trapped into thinking no one really understands the pain we are going through, so it is easier to just withdraw and isolate and hope for the best. We have seen the effects of this since we were forced to isolate during the pandemic. It has taken a toll, and mental health organizations are overwhelmed and understaffed. Primary care physicians are noting a rise in depression, anxiety, post-traumatic stress disorder (PTSD), and other mental health illnesses among the newly bereaved as well as among health-care workers. There are times when we need to be alone with our grief, but sharing our struggles also has value in bringing meaning to our experiences.

Key takeaways

> Tell your story to someone with a similar loss.
> Honor everyone's inherent dignity.
> Acknowledge other stories of loss.
> Find a way to connect with other grievers.
> Share in humanity to lessen suffering.
> When able, help another.

CHAPTER 8

Living Forward

....

You don't have to see the whole staircase, just take the first step.
—Martin Luther King Jr.

....

One expression often used in our culture when people tire of supporting others in their grief, "it's time to move on and live your life again," is not a popular one among the bereaved. It often brings more distress to them. This "moving on" suggests betrayal of the deceased for some mourners. Bereaved individuals do not want the grief to linger, but it does. They do not want to wake up to this "new normal," but they do. It's painful when your trusted support persons do not know how to be there for you. Therefore, I have emphasized the importance of solid and patient support persons who understand grief.

We need to have the right people by our side. When feelings and emotions are validated and acknowledged (instead of rushed, or worse yet, ignored altogether), our grief subsides naturally. The emotional pain does not disappear, but it is much more manageable.

In many ways, the pandemic and other world conditions have had a negative impact on those who are trying to process the grief from losing someone since 2020. As noted throughout this book, the uncertainty and fear surrounding the virus, coupled with an inability to feel safe in our world because of mass violence, continued racial tension, political division, and more has prolonged and even delayed our grief work. We have an altered grief to process, especially when we do not have the traditional support systems in place that we once knew. Many of our own close support persons are also grieving and trying to make sense of this changed world and are not as present to us, which makes our grief feel disenfranchised. Our perceived support was, and continues to be, weak.

Typically, finding a way to live forward with remembrance of who we lost takes time. As we have learned from the losses shared here, it's not an easy task when the loss is significant, such as your child or your spouse. On top of the usual challenges, our grief, as noted throughout this book, has been altered because of the continued uncertainty of the world we are inhabiting. When we feel fearful about what is happening with regard to our governance and our environment, for example, this distracts us from the normal working through of our loss. All of this alters a normal progression of grief as we set aside some of the processing of memories just to survive.

Many people ask me to tell them how to get through the grief in a healthy fashion, and they often anticipate that I hold a magical formula. This is understandable, as we live in an era where we know how to fix everything, and there is a specialist for every known ailment and experience in life. In the context of postmodern theories of bereavement, sociologist Tony Walter reminds us "it is all very well to say that everyone grieves differently, but people need to have some idea of what to expect when they or others, are grieving" (p. 208). This need to know what to expect as one moves through the loss is part of the ache in the process.

In my research study with widowed baby boomers, over half of the participants asked questions at the end of the interview such as "Do you think I am going to be okay?" These inquires came after answering some of my questions and telling me of their challenges in getting on with their lives. They were having little epiphanies during the two-hour interview. I also heard, "Why is this taking me so long?" and "I think I'm losing my mind." One criterion for participation in the study was that they had to be at least one year past the death, so most of them were concerned that they still felt the grief intensely and it was not letting up. It was also obvious that cultural expectations made their grief harder to process.

Some of the widows and widowers that I interviewed noted that they were afraid to live forward and likened it to abandonment of the spouse who died. "He was my superman, how can I move on?" One gentleman, when I asked him to tell me a little bit about himself (instead of diving right into the death of his wife) said, "There is no me. It was *us* for forty-two years." This shows an inability to even desire to live forward. He is just not ready to live life without his wife, even though this was year 3 post-loss.

These bereaved individuals were all attending grief support groups where they were learning skills and making new friends who carried the same heavy burden of the loss of a spouse. They were all in different years away from the death, which brought some relief to the new members. They were able to see that many people integrated the death and loss into their life narrative and lived life forward, even though they were still asking questions and editing their story.

The uncertainty in our world today takes away the cushion that typically makes the grief a bit easier to bear. COVID-19 stole that from us along with political turmoil, climate change, mass violence, racial tension, and overall uncertainty of the promise of a good future.

Looking ahead

In general terms, grieving is one of the most challenging life experiences, and people are ill prepared for it. And there is no guideline or manual to guide us. As twenty-first-century people, we google just about everything to provide us with instructions. And although there is a great deal of information online for grief, we must be careful, as misinformation from well-intended people is uploaded, yet they have no formal education or certification. They may have had a personal experience with death to share, but a caveat should be applied. It is not a one-size-fits-all template when we grieve loss. It's messy, and the process is not one that any one person can give a definitive guidebook of instructions for.

Nonetheless, here is my attempt based on my own experience as I grieved these family members. I like to use the analogy of car windshields and mirrors that, when used while driving, help you safely arrive at your destination. If we strive to live our lives by looking at what is ahead through the large front windshield, we will eventually, as we learn to carry the grief, find it helpful to look less in the past (the rearview mirror). We can, in due course, realize that there is so much life yet to live. These mirrors are all important, but there is a good reason the front windshield in a vehicle is so large and the rearview and side mirrors are small. We obviously need to use them all to arrive at our destination safely.

When driving, it is better to look at the road ahead, remembering to glance in the rearview mirror from time to time to see what is behind us. As is true in grief, looking back at our life with the deceased and moving through the memories are vital functions for a healthy outcome. However, using the front windshield and looking to the road ahead help us to avoid the possible hazards and potholes even if we cannot see them yet. Focusing on the road ahead ensures us that we can successfully get where we are going.

But we must also examine what holds us back. It could be feelings of regret or guilt in the rearview mirror that begin to haunt us. We can get distracted by the regret. Looking back too much can hinder our future. Even nostalgia has the potential to be an offender, as reliving the happy times too much brings only temporary help. When nostalgia is our daily companion, it can consume us and bring more sadness or becomes a detour that dead-ends.

Continuing the analogy, the side mirrors are equally important. They help us at times when we want to speed ahead, for example, while changing lanes or when backing up or parallel parking. Many people speed along roadsides without accessing the mirrors, but they are just as crucial for arriving safely at our destination. In grief, we can think of these side mirrors as our support persons. Knowing that they are always there provides us with a sense of security. We should use them on occasion. They (our support persons) should be firmly planted and identified. They help us to hold onto hope.

Reasonable hope

When we think of the concept of hope, we may find it hard to explain what it means, but we know we want it. There are so many reminders through our language and symbols that we ourselves and others continue to exhibit, such as "don't lose hope," "hold onto hope," and so on. But hope itself is black-and-white according to Kaethe Weingarten (2010) who reminds us that it admits no doubts, contradictions, or despair. Reasonable hope, on the other hand, she notes, "functions in a gray zone, where doubt, contradictions, and despair quite definitely coexist." She explains further that

> hope has a connotation of purity, whereas reasonable hope accepts that life can be messy. It embraces contradiction. Public life is rife with contradictions as is family life. Reasonable hope is easier to sustain since it does not get dashed, as innocent hope may, if contradictions emerge.

There are five characteristics used for considering this concept of reasonable hope when helping ourselves and others. It is relational (it flourishes in a relationship); consists of a practice (we do with others); maintains that the future is open, uncertain, and influenceable (embraces it); seeks goals and pathways to them (reforms goals and cultivates pathways); and accommodates doubt, contradictions, and despair (Weingarten 2010, p. 8).

Debra, our bereaved spouse, speaks to this idea of reasonable hope and the characteristic of embracing the future and its uncertainty.

> The hope that sustained my daughters and I is that we set out to keep Wade at home, and that we envisioned we would not have to put him in a

nursing home.... People kept telling me to check out these facilities, and when I did, I saw that what they tell you and show you is a "nice dining room," but I thought, "this isn't home, this isn't what I would call nice." I don't think extended family members realized how hard this was to maintain his care in our home with his type of dementia and all the possibilities we had to consider, such as the risk of violent attacks when the patient would not know who we were due to his dementia and nature of the illness.

We were fortunate to have kept him and ourselves safe (although one incident involved a police call for help). I can't even think about what a nursing home experience would have been like as I think about how much harder the grief would be now...but I was fortunate because the psychiatrist I was working with made it possible to some extent, as she provided an online portal for me to use for any urgent concerns, and they were very quick in getting back to me. I also held onto the reasonable hope that, after Wade was gone, I would have a few good years to do what it was I wanted to do with the rest of my life and regain the ability to live life freely without the heaviness of caregiving and so much unpredictability. This future life that I envisioned carried me through some very tough times in the years of caregiving. And, although it did not come to fruition, it served a purpose, and I'm glad I held onto it.

Wade died in July of 2020, so the landscape of Covid-19 ruined any possibility of travel, or other activities I had hoped to resume. And even now, to some extent, it is still very challenging, as the world seems to have changed so much and does not feel safe. The world I knew before he died is not here anymore. It's not just from the loss of my husband or even the pandemic but also all the social circumstances that I worked tirelessly to improve for others during my professional life as a social work counselor. Now, I can't seem to help myself, and I worry excessively about what kind of world my children and grandchildren will have. Before Wade's death, I never worried, so to speak. I may have had concern, but I was not an anxious or worried individual.

Right now, in fall of 2022, I am on an antidepressant as I took out my assessment tools and saw depression and did something proactive. On top of the processing of the loss, I think about many matters that are of great concern. We do not have a guarantee for a democracy or for help with climate change and issues of inequality among people, and this is all so troubling.

Our grief from these recent losses feels altered in so many ways. In order to live forward and carry our pain, we benefit from understanding that we must be reasonable in our expectations for the future years ahead. But when the world is seemingly falling apart around us, these circumstances modify our processing of grief. Again, we need to keep people in our lives who will help to provide us with realistic hope for the future, which ultimately cultivates resilience. These support persons should have a good understanding of grief and individual pathways in working through the death and the life changes it brings. If they are not beside us, we must identify and create the support ourselves, which may include a support group.

A word about resilience here, as I used to think *some* people were just genetically wired better than others to adapt to life circumstances. That is until I began to think about social conditions such as our educational level or access to resources that often are contributing factors in our ability to adapt to any adverse event. George

Bonanno's work in *The Other Side of Sadness: What the New Science of Bereavement Tells Us About Life After Loss* also helped.

Dr. Bonanno shares that we are *all* wired to some extent to survive.

> As I learned more about how people manage to withstand extremely aversive events, it became all the more apparent to me that humans are wired to survive. Not everybody manages well, but most of us do. And some of us, it seems, can deal with just about anything. We adapt, we change gears, we smile and laugh and do what we need to do, we nurture our memories, we tell ourselves it's not as bad as we thought, and before we know it, what once seemed bleak and bottomless has given way; the dark recedes and the sun once again peeks out from behind the clouds. (p. 81)

From black and white to color

It is important that we stay open to new possibilities as we carry our grief forward. I am reminded here as I write this last chapter of a woman in one of my research studies on widowhood. She noted how she was muddling her way through the agony of grief and watching her new grief support group friends in their bereavement. They (complete strangers) seemed to live what appeared to be a more vibrant life from this widow's perspective. Many of them participated in an annual cruise for widows and widowers arranged through the bereavement support agency. She was not drawn to it until year three into her grief when she decided to join them. To her surprise, she realized on the cruise ship that there was life yet to live. It was during the trip that her world went from "black and white to color." It was by no means the same life, but she regained the hope to live forward. For such a long time, she had thought that if she was happy in her new "bereaved life" now, it might reflect some measure of disrespect to her deceased spouse.

Prior to attending the support group, she had watched close friends who lost their spouses. They remained low-key and sad for the first few years. She had remembered that and felt a strong need to emulate their behavior. Fortunately, she went on the cruise to learn otherwise and began to refocus her perspective on living forward. She realized that she had been just existing and not really living.

Oftentimes, our perspective for our own grief journey is distorted based on cultural messages or from our limited exposure to grief. For example, bereaved spouses are told not to make any major decisions in the first year of bereavement. However, some people find themselves in a financial situation that they cannot sustain, especially if the spouse died young and unexpectedly. Women might feel overwhelmed with all the maintenance of a home, whereas men may find meal planning, cooking, and cleaning to be a large part of their distress. Regardless, we must make decisions that will ease our grief and anxiety. These are not easy decisions, so I encourage those having to make them to seek out trusted individuals to help look at all the pros and cons. This step involves having some compassion for our grieving selves as we move through the grief to gain the joy in our hearts again. It is okay to need and seek out the help of trusted individuals to assist us in the love we need to cultivate for ourselves while still bringing honor to the deceased through legacy.

Integrating legacy

To bring wholeness back into our fractured and disrupted selves, we have found ways to integrate our deceased loved ones' legacies into our lives with remembrance. Each one of their lives and personalities brought remarkable richness into our families, and we honor and remember them as we move onward through life.

We use Tupelo honey regularly in memory of our niece Anna, as she loved honey and the song by Van Morrison, which was played at her memorial service. We wear her bandana on occasion that was given to us by her parents after we wore them at her service (that she sported proudly in her daily life). Her mother, as shared earlier, has dance parties with her aunt by phone every Friday night to remember the fun they had together, as that was their routine for decades.

We honor Wade by helping others as he always showed a quick response to help anyone and everyone without questioning their unfortunate circumstances. We joke about his handkerchiefs (and saved a few), as he always offered you his current one as a gesture of kindness, if needed. We talk about his driving and the wild rides he gave us when he was well, and then during his dementia when we were unsuccessful in getting the keys away from him. As a former police officer, his routine at work involved a great deal of driving. In his illness, the fast driving seemed to calm him, yet his eighty-mile-an-hour drives in a fifty-five-mile-per-hour zone filled us with terror.

We try to incorporate our mother Anna's unconditional love for all people by listening intently to others (especially the marginalized) and praying for all people, even for those who challenge us. Her nickname was Annie Sparkle because her beautiful blue eyes had an inviting liveliness that drew you in and her sense of fashion was remarkable. We attempt to add a little sparkle to our lives and to that of others, in numerous ways, as she did so often in her stylish way.

For Mom, we also visit her grave, take flowers, and stay in touch with some of her friends who were so kind to her. Recently, I took my young granddaughters to the cemetery where we spread out a blanket near her headstone and had a little picnic on a sunny summer day. We reminisced about their visits with their great-grandmother, which were frequent, especially near the end of her life. I am gently trying to teach them to hold onto memories but live forward with remembrance.

We honor and remember our brother, Mark, by retelling his corny jokes or talking about his Donald Duck imitation that always made the room explode with laughter. We think of him at the northern cabin where he liked to hunt and fish and visited often. His deer blind is up, and reminders of the happy memories made at the cabin are displayed through plaques and other memorabilia along the walls.

Our goal through these many gestures and practices is to show that our family members were cherished and will not be forgotten.

And that notion alone is very comforting to us. Remembrance brings the disruption from the death some meaning and order. Ritual and remembrance aid our grieving journeys. We remember through the telling of stories or through memorial services on the anniversary of the death. Although challenging emotionally, they are cathartic in the long run.

Ritual gives us a gentle push into acceptance of the reality of the loss. We can create our own ceremonies and construct our stories of the deceased, or we can attend larger group gatherings held in communities. After the death, ritual and remembrance continue to cultivate resilience, as loss challenges us to relearn our world without the deceased in it.

Grieving is an active adjustment to a new and changed land-scape, where our relationship with the deceased also takes new form, from the physical to the spiritual, that often includes some level of suffering. Holding on to reasonable hope, keeping a circle of strong support persons, and practicing quieting the mind will also sustain us in our new world without those we loved and lost. For Christian family members, this means the hope of seeing them again in eternal life.

Most importantly, loving yourself and accepting your limitations as a human being are elements of self-compassion, both tools that need a place in your self-care tool kit that should be utilized daily. Live forward with remembrance and embrace the peace that was meant to be, the peace that I believe only God can give. Carry on the legacy of the ones lost and develop a new bond.

Continuing bonds with the deceased

Previous excerpts show that the strong physical bond mom Maureen had with her daughter Anna has vanished. But I admire her for how she has shifted that bond (to continue it in a new way). I am reminded of the "continuing bonds theory" we use among helping professionals who work with the bereaved. It was developed by Klass, Silverman, and Nickman to suggest a new archetype where instead of detaching from the one who died, we create a new bond or relationship with them. This is where you find ways to continue some

117

type of connection with the one who died as you move along in your grief. So you have to redefine the relationship over your life course.

Death does not mean the end of a relationship, but a change in the relationship, "with new dimensions and possibilities" (Klass, Silverman, and Nickman 1996, xix). Mom Maureen continues her bond with her deceased daughter by scheduling the Friday night dance parties to recollect what she had with her when she was alive.

In some ways, we have all continued a bond with the deceased, through remembrance. We visit cemeteries, donate in the name of the deceased, talk to them, and so forth. Grief counselors and helping professionals no longer encourage the bereaved to let go or detach from the relationship to the deceased, as we have learned that it is natural and normal to have a bond even after death.

For me, I wear my mother's jewelry and feel her presence when I do. I keep various personal items of hers close, and when I find myself in distress, I ask Mom to pray with me. You can also write letters to those who died, keep photos up and tell others about who they were, finish something they started such as a project, take on a hobby they had, or volunteer somewhere they cherished, and the like.

Also, other connections you once had because of the deceased can be hard to replace, which creates yet another form of emptiness. Mom Maureen tells us here with respect to the relationship she held with professionals who also cared for her daughter:

> I was my daughter's caretaker her entire life, but she was mine as well. I often tell people that I needed her more than she needed me. In the months since I lost her, I myself have been lost. My life revolved around her. Her medical team, her staff at the adult day program she attended, her friends were my social circle. I adored each and every one of them. My daughter was my connection with these people. I know that they all hold my daughter's memory close, but our lives have gone in different directions…they, too, are now gone from my life.

There should be some way to keep a connection for the bereaved parents with those who provided care to a family member for decades. Perhaps a specific support group designed for those who have lost this 24-7 role of caregiving would fill a gap for a unique set of grievers in our society. Moving forward can be much more challenging when we consider all the secondary losses due to other bonds severed abruptly.

Key takeaways

Look ahead (front windshield) but also glance at the past (rear-view mirror).

Keep strong support persons close (side mirrors).

Hold onto reasonable hope.

Look at new possibilities (change your perspective).

Be kind to yourself.

Create and integrate legacy for the deceased.

Live forward with remembrance.

Embrace peace.

CONCLUDING REMARKS

What we have once enjoyed and deeply loved we can never
lose, for all that we love deeply becomes a part of us.
—Helen Keller

....

The year 2020 was, and still is, a blur, but I want to preserve our stories to show the strength, resilience, and transformation that can come out of the great suffering and emptiness loss often brings. The accumulated family losses were intensely felt as many of us moved through a reflection period, one where we learned to adapt to the absence of those we loved.

The year 2021 was an enormous adjustment for our family with the changes to our lives because of the losses from death and the additional chaos of a changed global landscape due to the pandemic. As we headed into 2022, yet another variant of the virus continued to disrupt our lives. Between the grief we carried, the global chaos of the pandemic, the divisions in families over politics, climate change that has brought numerous natural disasters, racial unrest, war, and mass shootings of innocent people, our emotions have run the gamut. Many of these same concerns, except for the pandemic, were noted in my 1972 story of loss and change in Chapter 1. This past three-year time frame in our twenty-first century involved long-suffering as we sorted through the multiple losses, supported one another, and figured out how to live anew in a changed world.

As we continue to move forward with our losses, our family has learned valuable lessons as put forth in these chapters. First, to be grateful (for something or someone) and to be gentle with ourselves and others. For me, I have written here about how being stricken with grief is challenging yet life changing. I highlight the importance of focusing on how these experiences have the potential to transform us into better human beings. After the news, the disruption, all the suffering and emptiness, we can learn to be still, to contemplate, to surrender and finally allow for the experience to transform us. This movement eventually led us to a place of giving back and helping others with the lessons from our newfound experiences.

Regardless of how we process the loss, we must all find a way to move toward whatever life is left and expect some good to come. Our family's primary goal became one of helping others as we shared our pain and struggle, our triumphs, and our setbacks.

This writing, as noted earlier on, is not intended to be a guideline, but rather an account of personal grief experiences. It does, however, capture some great takeaways based on the work of many scholars. Their work has reminded me of how we need to lean into and feel the pain of our losses, accept them, and then start to open our minds to a future that looks hopeful.

As we muster strength to "live forward," we also carry all those we lost with us. They are weaved into our own life narratives. And so I invite you to tell your story and to invite others to tell you about someone they loved and lost and about their life and death stories.

In the context of my faith life, I pray for their souls and for their intercession for us on earth. Anna Louise, Wade, Anna Marie, and Mark will never be forgotten, and we are forever changed by the lives they lived and by their deaths. We want them to be remembered, and so we integrate their life and death stories into our own narrative.

We are learning to carry sorrow alongside joy and live out the rest of our lives with hopefulness. We carry hope that we can reunite with those we loved and are now gone from earth. Although many of us can still relate to being *grief-stricken*, we believe that by sharing our stories, the losses have more meaning and purpose. May you find your way through grief while also helping others as you live forward with remembrance of those you lost.

POSTSCRIPT UPDATE

Postscript Update: Mom, Maureen on the loss of her daughter Anna Louise

Q1: What has this experience been like for you to share part of your loss story in *Grief-Stricken*?

Throughout my daughter's life, I was her voice, her interpreter. Anna was nonverbal but certainly not silent. In a way, Anna was speaking a language that only I could translate. I was honored to be her voice. I observed and attempted to share with others what I thought she was trying to communicate with her vocalizations and body language. Through this book project, I was able to share her life and her impact on others. I feel grateful that this book will help preserve Anna's legacy as a unique, fierce, beautiful, and powerful spirit.

On the other hand, writing about her death (I still have trouble using that word) has frequently been traumatic for me. As a parent, even though my Anna had profound special needs, I never once entertained the possibility that she would die before I did. She was just too tough, too resilient. Until she wasn't. Recounting the events of her last moments on earth, scrolling through pictures of her on my phone for publication, and walking through my too-quiet home as I searched for the right words to do her memory justice often trigger a tsunami of grief and sorrow.

I save in my Notes app on my phone phrases that I have read about grief and loss. I found the words of author Megan

Devine to be spot on, from her book *It's OK That You're Not OK: Meeting Grief and Loss in a Culture That Doesn't Understand:*

> "Grief is simply love in its most wild and painful form."

I learned through writing about Anna that grief is my partner. It is often a paralyzing force that literally stops me in my tracks. On the other hand, my grief is a reminder that I was blessed with the deepest, most profound love I could ever experience. If that is the tradeoff, I'll take it.

Q2: What one piece of advice do you have for the reader to consider when it comes to supporting a bereaved parent?

Allow the bereaved to grieve as they choose. Don't try to direct or define their grief.

Don't take their silence as rejection. Reach out at unexpected times to let them know you're thinking about them. If you don't get a response, it's okay. They got the message that you care about them and their well-being.

Q3: What was the least helpful to you as you processed the death of your daughter, Anna Louise?

I was stunned and hurt by people who expected me to move on and resume a life that I could never get back. I am not the same person I was. I will never return to being that person. I will never *move on*.

Q4: As you are processing this loss, what are you, or others, doing now to create a legacy for Anna Louise?

Our family just observed the third anniversary of Anna's passing. Since losing her, I have had great difficulty going out in public. I am profoundly uncomfortable being in the *real world*. However, this year I decided to be brave. I took Anna's brother and his fiancée to a concert by one of Anna's favorite artists. I tried to conjure her spirit as I watched the performance. I pictured in my mind her reaction to the music.

I go into Anna's room every morning. I greet her with a "good morning, sunshine girl" or "good morning, princess girl," open her shades, and turn on her music. I tell her how much I love her. I kiss her pillow. I tell her how much I miss her.

Anna and I used to celebrate the end of the week with a girls' dance party. My sister and I take turns choosing a song of the week and send it to each other to carry on the tradition.

Anna had the most beautiful hair that I loved combing and styling into a ponytail. I began finding random hair ties on walks, runs, or even while going to the store. I like to believe that Anna is letting me know that her spirit is still present, and they are a sign from her. I have a dresser full of pictures of her and a special box where I keep all the hair ties. I thank her every time I find one.

I have also started sending boxes of Anna's Gourmet Goodies, baked goods, to people who have had an impact on my life that year. I do it in honor of Anna.

Postscript Update: Dad, Jeff on the loss of his daughter Anna Louise

Q1: What has this experience been like for you to share part of your loss story in *Grief-Stricken*?

It has been difficult but cathartic for sure. It is good to talk about my feelings of loss. Hopefully it will help others to understand that it's okay to let others know you are sad, hurting, and missing your loved one. Don't ever try to *get over it*.

Q2: What one piece of advice do you have for the reader to consider when it comes to supporting a bereaved parent?

Be patient with those grieving, and don't try to force a timeline for someone to get over a loss. Do not use coined phrases such as, "Well, they are in a better place" or "God only gives you what you can deal with."

Q3: What was the least helpful to you as you processed the death of your daughter, Anna Louise?

Least helpful? When people forget about you and your loss when they stop checking in on you. When they expect you to suddenly *get over it*. When they never bring it up ever. It is a large part of my everyday life, and it helps if people ask me occasionally how I am dealing with my grief and loss. It also helps me to know that they are remembering our daughter.

Q4: As you are processing this loss, what are you, or others, doing now to create a legacy for Anna Louise?

Our home is filled with my daughter's art. We talk about it, and we find small daily ways to remember her. We think about what we do in our daily routine and try to keep Anna's part in that.

Postscript Update: Debra on the loss of her husband, Wade Edward

Q1: What has this experience been like for you to share part of your loss story in *Grief-Stricken*?

I participated in this book project in the hope that there is something useful for someone else out there from sharing my story. I also want to let people know that there are ways that you can keep patients with Lewy body dementia at home for the course of the illness if you have the right support and resources as I did. There are better options than assisted living, and I was fortunate, as well as my husband, to be able to have them and benefit from them.

Q2: What one piece of advice do you have for the reader to consider when it comes to supporting a bereaved widow?

My advice to others when trying to support a bereaved spouse would be to follow their lead. If they want time alone, let them be. If they want to talk, then be ready to listen. But support them without giving advice, unless they specifically ask for it.

Q3: What was the least helpful to you as you processed the death of your husband, Wade Edward?

I think for me, the least helpful thing in this whole experience was not about the death but rather during the long years of caregiving. I had a lot of guilt in anticipating his death because I wanted all the stress to be gone, but this meant the end for him. I was worn out and feeling bad for him and for myself. It was a bit of a double-edged sword because you want them to live on, the ill spouse, but not in this way. So all of this lingering and constant self-inflicted guilt was of little help as I processed what was to come.

After the death, it was not helpful to be in the midst of a pandemic. The limitations to developing a new routine were frustrating. I was on lockdown by myself. We had been in lockdown during his illness, but I was busy with caregiving, and my husband, in some sense, was still with me. Afterward, I thought I would get my life back, but I did not.

Q4: As you are processing this loss, what are you, or others, doing now to create a legacy for Wade Edward?

We continue to support the things that were so important to him. He loved being there for family and especially for the grandkids, so I have picked up where he left off. I was always there too, but now his presence is greatly missed. I also support, through donations, those organizations that he did, such as Special Olympics and Catholic schools. I guess you could say that I am emulating his values. We had similar ones, but he was over the top in his responses and thoroughly enjoyed all of it, and I will honor his legacy by remembering his values and acting on them.

Postscript Update: author on the loss of her mother, Anna Marie

Q1: What has this experience been like for you to share part of your loss story in *Grief-Stricken*?

It has been surreal as I never thought I would be writing a book without the love and support of my beloved mother. She was such a vital part of my life for six and a half decades. This experience really sharpened my realization of what she meant to me.

Q2: What one piece of advice do you have for the reader to consider when it comes to supporting a bereaved adult child?

Know that regardless of the circumstances, it is helpful to ask them about the parent they lost and be willing to listen to their story, without judgment.

Q3: What was the least helpful to you as you processed the death of your mother, Anna Marie?

The least helpful to me was when people would under-value my grief experience because my mom *lived a long life*. I was told I should be grateful that I had her for so long. I was! I got that response a lot, and it was not helpful; rather, it was dismissive of the grief I was processing over losing my beloved mom. One other note, because of fractured family relation-ships, it was disappointing not to move through the memories of Mom with people I had expected to. It would have been helpful to reminisce with them on important dates, such as her birthday, Mother's Day, and St. Patrick's Day (because she loved being Irish and celebrating it). An occasional text was not what I had expected. Perhaps a voice text would have been nice. I was able to grieve with close others, but it was not the same as they had a different relationship with Mom than those whom I had expected would be grieving alongside me.

Q4: As you are processing this loss, what are you, or others, doing now to create a legacy for your mom, Anna Marie?

We, my husband and I, continue to keep in contact with some of her good friends and her pastor. We also carry on her values, which include praying for the ordained religious priests among us, practicing the faith she passed on, and living a selfless and simple life.

Postscript Update: Kevin on the loss of his brother, Mark Thomas

Q1: What has this experience been like for you to share part of your loss story in *Grief-Stricken*?

It has been helpful to be able to talk about the loss of Mark and know that it is being shared widely. It gives me some peace of mind to know that others will now know an incredible human being, my brother, along with his contributions.

Q2: What one piece of advice do you have for the reader to consider when it comes to supporting a bereaved sibling?

That it helps greatly if people can tell the surviving sibling stories about the deceased. I felt much better knowing the positive influence my brother had in the lives of others.

Q3: What was the least helpful to you as you processed the death of Mark, your brother?

Not being able to have a proper funeral that we were accustomed to in pre-COVID days. As I said in an excerpt earlier, it was like a chapter without an ending after his funeral Mass when we could not gather to share stories and comfort each other.

Q4: As you are processing this loss, what are you, or others, doing now to create a legacy for Mark?

One thing not noted in the book that was an important contribution to his legacy is that my wife and I purchased children's books on a topic dear to him, wild birds, and donated them to his local library in the town he resided in. We added bookplates with his name on each of them. I know he would have loved that as he loved children and enjoyed bird-watching with them. We also pray for him and the other deceased family members in our daily prayer time.

REFERENCES

Bach, M. 1965. *The Power of Perception: How Life Rewards Those Willing to Look for the Unseen, Listen for the Unheard in Search for a Richer, More Meaningful Existence.* New York: Hawthorn Books, Inc.

Bogle, A. M. and S. Go. 2015. Breaking Bad (News) Death-Telling in the Emergency Department. *Missouri Medicine* 112 (1): 12–16.

Bonanno, G. A. 2009. *The Other Side of Sadness: What the New Science of Bereavement Tells Us about Life after Loss.* Basic Books, a Member of the Perseus Books Group.

Boss, P. 2000. *Ambiguous Loss.* Harvard University Press.

Brach, T. 2021. *Trusting the Gold: Uncovering Your Natural Goodness.* Sounds True Publishing.

Brooks, D. "What Do You Say to the Sufferer?" *New York Times*, December 9, 2021, op-ed.

Brooks, D. 2020. *The Second Mountain: The Quest for a Moral Life.* Random House.

Cohen, O. and M. Katz. 2015. "Grief and Growth of Bereaved Siblings as Related to Attachment Style and Flexibility." *Death Studies* 39 (3): 158–164. https://doi.org/10.1080/07481187.2014.923069.

Doka, K. J. and T. L. Martin. 1999. *Men Don't Cry, Women Do: Transcending Gender Stereotypes of Grief (Series in Death, Dying, and Bereavement)*, First Edition. Routledge.

Durkheim, E. 1895. *The Rules of Sociological Method.* New York: Free Press.

Frank, A. W. 1995. *The Wounded Storyteller: Body, Illness and Ethics.* Chicago: Chicago University Press.

Fredrickson, B. L. 2001. "The Role of Positive Emotions in Positive Psychology: The Broaden-and-Build Theory of Positive Emotions." *American Psychologist,* 56: 218–226.

Giddens, Anthony. 1991. *Modernity and Self-Identity.* Cambridge: Polity Press.

Gillies, J., and R. A. Neimeyer. 2006. "Loss, Grief, and the Search for Significance: Toward a Model of Meaning Reconstruction in Bereavement." *Journal of Constructivist Psychology,* 19: 31–65.

Hicks, D., 2021. *Dignity: Its Essential Role in Resolving Conflict.* Yale University Press.

Horwitz, A.V. & Wakefield, J.C., 2012. *The Loss of Sadness: How Psychiatry Transformed Normal Sorrow into Depressive Disorder.* Oxford University Press.

Hoy, W. 2013. *Do Funerals Matter? The Purposes and Practices of Death Rituals in Global Perspective.* Routledge.

Janoff-Bulman, R. 1992. *Shattered Assumptions.* New York, NY: Free Press.

Keating, T., W. Meninger, and B. Pennington. Centering Prayer App. Centering Prayer—Apps on Google Play.

Klass D., P. R. Silverman, and S. L. Nickman, eds. 1996. *Continuing Bonds: New Understandings of Grief.* Philadelphia: Taylor & Francis.

Krupp, J., Rev. Fr. 2021. Church of the Holy Family, Grand Blanc, Michigan. Feast of the Holy Family Jesus, Mary & Joseph. December 26, 2021. Sermon. https://www.facebook.com/HolyFamilyGrandBlanc/videos/729807004659730.

Kurtz, J. and S. Lyubomirsky. 2008. Chapter 2, "Toward a Durable Happiness." In *Pursuing Human Flourishing,* edited by Lopez, 21–36. Praeger Publishers.

LaGrand, Louis E. 2006. *Love Lives On: Learning from the Extraordinary Encounters of the Bereaved.* Berkley Publishing.

Lord, J.H., & Stewart, A.E., 2008, *I'll Never Forget Those Words: A Practical Guide to Death Notification.* Compassion Press.

Lyubomirsky, S., L. King, and E. Diener. 2005. "The Benefits of Frequent Positive Affect: Does Happiness lead to Success?" *Psychological Bulletin*, 131: 803–855. https://doi.org/10.1037/0033-2909.131.6.803

Marris, P. 1974. 2014. *Loss and Change.* Pantheon Books.

National Center for Faculty Development & Diversity. 2022. Monday Motivator. *Reckoning with Resistance.* Tips from the NCFDD Monday Motivator: December 2022 edition (ucsb.edu).

Neimeyer, R. A. 2001. "Reauthoring Life Narratives: Grief Therapy as Meaning Reconstruction." *Israel Journal of Psychiatry and Related Sciences*, 38: 171–183.

New York Times. 2002. *Portraits 9/11/01. The Collected Portraits of Grief.* New York: Times Books.

Nicholson, L. (2006). *Living on the seabed: A memoir of love, life and survival.* London: Vermilion

Parkes C. M. (1988). Bereavement as a psychosocial transition: Process of adaptation to change. *Journal of Social Issues,* 44, 53–65.

Piliavin, J. A. 2003. "Doing Well by Doing Good: Benefits for the Benefactor." In *Flourishing: Positive Psychology and the Life Well Lived*, edited by C. L. M. Keyes and J. Haidt, 227–247. Washington, DC: American Psychological Association.

Renzenbrink, I. 2010. *Fluttering on Fences: Stories of Loss and Change.* Anna B. quote, p. 43. Lakeside Education and Training.

Rohr, R. 2011. *Falling Upward: A Spirituality for the Two Halves of Life.* Jossey-Bass.

Shear, K. Social Impact LIVE: *Loss and Grief During the Coronavirus Pandemic.* You Tube Video presented in April of 2020 by Columbia School of Social Work. https://www.youtube.com/watch?v=nVmQdQTJHW4.

Sheen, F. J., 1982. *Treasure in Clay. The Autobiography of Fulton J. Sheen.* Image.

Siegel, D. *Name It to Tame It.* Mindful Awareness Research Center at UCLA. Name It to Tame It: Label Your Emotions to Overcome Negative Thoughts | Mindfulness.com. Retrieved from https://mindfulness.com/mindful-living/name-it-to-tame-it.

Smith, H. I. 1994. *On Grieving the Death of a Father.* Augsburg Fortress.

Stroebe, M. and H. Schut. 1999. "The Dual Process Model of Coping with Bereavement: Rationale and Description." *Death Studies* 23 (3): 197–224.

Vredevelt, P. 1984. *Empty Arms: Emotional Support for Those Who Have Suffered Miscarriage or Stillbirth.* Multnomah Press.

Walter, T. 2001. *On Bereavement: The Culture of Grief.* Open University Press.

Weingarten, K. 2010. "Reasonable Hope: Construct, Clinical Applications, and Supports." *Family Process* 49 (1): 5–25. doi: 10.1111/j.1545-5300.2010.01305.x.

Winfrey, O. *Inspiration.* 100+ Empowering Oprah Winfrey Quotes for Success. Retrieved from 50 Inspirational Oprah Winfrey Quotes on Success | AwakenTheGreatnessWithin.

ABOUT THE AUTHOR

 Laurel Elizabeth Hilliker, PhD, FT is a sociologist with sixteen years of experience as a collegiate lecturer in both sociology and public health courses. She earned two graduate degrees in sociology, a master of arts degree and a doctorate in philosophy from Michigan State University with a concentration in health and well-being and a specialization in grief and bereavement studies. She holds a fellow in thanatology through the Association for Death Education and Counseling. Her work has appeared in *Faith Catholic Magazine* as well as in scholarly journals including *Death Studies*; *Illness, Crisis & Loss*; *Omega, Journal of Death Studies;* and *Bereavement Care: An International Journal for Those Who Help Bereaved People.* She developed a college-level course for both undergraduate and graduate students, *Wellness in the Face of Loss*, which she teaches annually. Guest lectures and speaking engagements are provided through her own consulting firm, *Bearing Loss: Grief Education and Consulting, LLC,* which is the result of her continued desire to provide education for the bereaved and their families, as well as for the professionals who assist them. Dr. Hilliker is also an expert contributor to Help Texts, which provides mental health and grief support through text messages. She lives in Michigan with her husband, Kevin.

Printed in the USA
CPSIA information can be obtained
at www.ICGtesting.com
LVHW031122230224
772606LV00042B/642